MAKE CREATURES
WITH FELT MISTRESS

MAKE CREATURES
WITH FELT MISTRESS

12 COUTURE CHARACTERS TO SEW

LOUISE EVANS

LAURENCE KING PUBLISHING

LAURENCE KING

First published in 2016
by Laurence King Publishing Ltd
361–373 City Road
London EC1V 1LR
Tel: +44 20 7841 6900
Fax: +44 20 7841 6910
email: enquiries@laurenceking.com
www.laurenceking.com

A catalogue record for this book is available
from the British Library

ISBN: 978 1 78067 827 6

Design: Charlie Bolton, Jane Chipchase, Mark Holt, The
Urban Ant
Photography by Simon Pask except photographs on pages
7, 9 and 10 courtesy of Louise Evans.
Character illustrations by Jonathan Edwards, except for
Corney Island Dawg, illustrations by Jon Burgerman, and
Beardo, illustrations by Pete Fowler
Step-by-step sewing illustrations by The Urban Ant

Printed in China

CONTENTS

INTRODUCTION

I started sewing at a very early age (there's still a tiny rabbit in 1970s towelling somewhere in my mum's house!). As a child I was never happy unless I was making something. I would do my best to assist my mum when she was making small fundraising items for our local nursery school, attempt to make everything they made on Blue Peter (sorry, mum, for emptying an entire bottle of washing-up liquid down the sink because I needed the bottle) and spend hours with my dad, a joiner, building go-karts in his shed. If you've never seen a go-kart 'pimped' by a seven-year-old then you're missing out!

I knew I wanted to make things for a living but I was unaware of what job I could get that would scratch that itch. I left school and started to work for Laura Ashley as a seamstress. I learned a lot about construction and quality (they were extremely strict!) but soon began to make plans to go to university and learn more about design. During my years at university I met two people who would prove to be a great influence on my life: Peter, who taught pattern drafting and fabric manipulation (I still use similar techniques when working out how to make a flat fabric into a 3D shape, and clothing is a big part of my characters too),

and Mrs Payne, my very, very strict millinery teacher. I wanted to make hats but my university didn't teach millinery, so I arranged private lessons with Mrs Payne, an elderly lady who had spent her life making hats. I would spend hours stitching something, but if the stitches weren't perfect she wouldn't hesitate to make me undo them and start again. I have her to thank for my patience when hand sewing (and also my hatred of using glue on fabric).

After I graduated I worked for over 10 years as a bespoke dressmaker, predominantly on wedding dresses. I made dresses for clients of all shapes and sizes. This experience really helped when I started making clothes for creatures. I'd always made characters for friends as birthday presents, but never thought it could be a full-time career. Due to a serendipitous tweet, my work was spotted by a fashion boutique, who wanted me to fill their window for London Fashion Week. This led almost directly to having my own Christmas window in Selfridges' iconic Oxford Street store in London. I haven't really looked back since then. I now work full-time making creatures and characters, with the very occasional wedding dress for friends or special clients. I work alongside my partner Jonathan, an illustrator, producing characters for editorials, advertising, music videos, fashion shoots and films, and we also exhibit our work internationally.

A lot of our characters are based on people we have encountered or seen while we are out and about. We're always nudging each other when we see someone with a distinctive look that would work when styling some of our pieces. We love to travel, which is always inspiring. Jonathan is constantly sketching and I like to buy fabrics from our travels that can be used for new pieces.

I never really draw, except maybe a scrawled attempt to explain something to Jonathan. Jonathan always does the 2D and I always do the 3D. How the characters start differs from piece to piece. Sometimes they are made straight from a completely finished sketch by Jonathan; other times they start from a piece of fabric or 3D fabric shape. The process is fairly organic. We have worked together for so long that we understand each other's work very well.

If I have one piece of advice when making something, it's never give up halfway through. Even if it looks as though it's going all wrong, carry on. I can't count the amount of times I have started a project and then thought 'I hate this' halfway through, ready to consign it to the scrap heap, and Jonathan has convinced me to carry on. Those kinds of pieces always seem to end up being some of my favourites once they are finished.

We have picked a selection of characters to share with you in this book, including two designed by Pete Fowler and Jon Burgerman, both brilliant artists and good friends of mine who I have collaborated with many times over the years.

Right, it's all very well sitting here reading this, but you have characters to make, so come on – get stitching!

TOOLS AND MATERIALS

THREAD

A good-quality thread for machine and hand sewing is important. For attaching limbs, and for any other areas where stitches need to be pulled tight, an extra-strong thread should be used – there is nothing more annoying than having a thread snap on you. When pieces change colour along a seam (for example Corney Island Dawg's boots/legs), always change to a matching colour of thread for each section; this will make your finished piece much smarter.

TOOLS

Besides needles and thread, the tools I can't live without are:
- Sharp scissors (large and small)
- Bradawl
- Chopstick
- Medical forceps
- Long-nose pliers
- Tailor's chalk
- Teazel brush

I can't wear a thimble but if you can get used to wearing one, metal or leather, your fingers will thank you.

CUTTING THE PAPER PATTERNS

Trace the paper patterns you need for each project carefully, making sure you transfer all information such as eye placement and pile/grain lines for fur and dress fabrics. Felt has no grain, so it can be cut any way. Always lay the paper patterns onto the fabric to check the best layout before you cut, also making sure you cut opposites where needed. It's so annoying if you run out of fabric because of careless cutting (I speak from experience).

CUTTING FABRIC FOR CLOTHING

Either pin the paper pattern to the fabric or mark around the pattern with tailor's chalk. Use pinking shears to cut out clothing pieces because this looks neater if the raw edges won't be overlocked (serged). Stitch with a sewing machine and a straight stitch. If the fabrics you are using are very stretchy use a very slight zigzag, or the stretch stitch setting on your sewing machine.

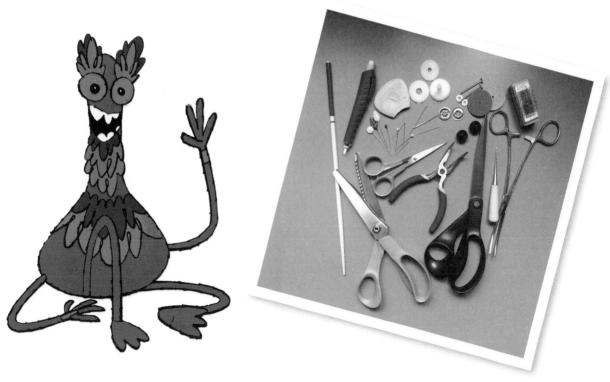

FABRICS

FELT

The four main types of felt available are wool felt, wool blend (usually either 30% or 40% wool mixed with viscose), acrylic felt and polyester felt. As you would expect, wool felt is the most expensive and polyester the cheapest. Most craft shops sell felt in either squares or rectangles (and it's usually manmade felt), but you can buy felt by the metre online and from bigger fabric stores. I usually use wool felt or acrylic felt. I avoid the really cheap polyester felt, as I find it a bit thin and easily damaged.

I usually pin the paper pattern to the felt and then cut around that, but if you prefer you can mark around the paper pattern with a fabric pencil or tailor's chalk. If you use a normal ink pen or a pencil be sure to cut just inside the pen line so the pen marks are cut away.

Felt is straightforward to stitch, but can be easily stretched out of shape when handled, so be careful when turning pieces to the right side and when stuffing. Always run a line of machine stitches (stay stitches) along the edges left open for stuffing. This will prevent the edges stretching and make it a lot easier for you to hand stitch the gap later.

FAKE FUR

Take note of the direction of the pile and always position pattern pieces with the pile direction as marked.

Mark around patterns with tailor's chalk or pencil, then carefully make shallow cuts with scissors so you only cut through the backing and don't harm the long fur fibres.

Always stitch down with the direction of the pile. This may mean you have to turn the piece over, once you have sewn one half, to sew the other side.

Use the edge of your scissors or a long pin to tuck all fibres inwards when stitching seams.

Use a pin or invest in a teazel brush (a wire brush, specially for making fur toys) to release caught fur fibres from seams.

When you are stitching fur it will slip because of the pile. Use pins or tacking stitches to hold and match balance notches (as marked on the pattern pieces) to check that no slippage has occurred.

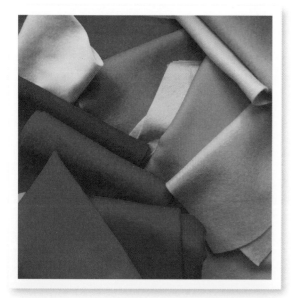

STITCHING AND STUFFING

STITCHES

Straight machine stitch, or back stitch if sewing by hand.

Slip stitch/oversew (by hand) to attach felt layers such as eyes, frills, teeth and mouth.

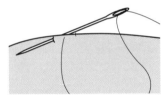

Ladder stitch to join gaps left open for stuffing, attaching limbs, horns etc.

STITCHING TIPS

- When stitching over darts or any other seams, open them first, because this will prevent bulk when turned through to the other side.

- Seam allowances are usually 1cm (⅜in), but with smaller pattern pieces this differs. Refer to the markings on the paper patterns.

- Nick into all curved seams so that when they are turned right side out the curve is nice and smooth, with no puckering or bulkiness.

- For a neat point, clip all corners before turning right side out.

- Opposites: always cut and sew opposite shapes of things like feet, hands and arms, so you finish with a pair.

PRESSING

When pressing seams open, or pressing collars and finished clothes, take care not to over-press. Use a pressing cloth (an old piece of cotton or cotton calico) between the iron and the clothes, or you will easily damage or ruin the look of a piece.

STUFFING

When stuffing felt be careful not to overstuff and force the felt out of shape. Make sure the stuffing fills all spaces and is evenly distributed, checking the shaping of your piece as you go. It is easy to ruin a piece by either under- or overstuffing. Use a chopstick or medical forceps to push the stuffing into tricky areas. When stuffing legs that are still open at both ends, make sure the stuffing is firm enough – once you have sewn one of the ends it's a good idea to push the stuffing up a bit to make sure.

JOINTS

There are two main types of joints, a cotter pin joint and a plastic safety joint. They can both be inserted into the top edge of the arm or the top side of the arm, depending on the figure you are making.

COTTER PIN JOINTS

These are made up of two wooden discs, two metal washers and a metal cotter pin.

Push the cotter pin through one of the metal washers, then one of wooden discs.

Place the wooden disc with the cotter pin sticking out into the top edge of the arm and use running stitch to tightly gather up the edge of the arm round the cotter pin. Secure the stitching.

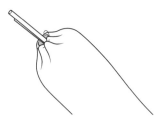

Push the cotter pin (now firmly attached to the arm) through the hole in the body made for the arm placement (marked on paper patterns) from the outside in. On the inside, thread on the other wooden disc and metal washer.

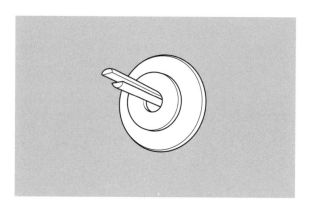

With a pair of long-nose pliers, separate each pin outwards and into a curl. The tighter the curl, the stiffer the joint.

PLASTIC SAFETY JOINTS

These are made up of a plastic joint, a washer and a locking washer.

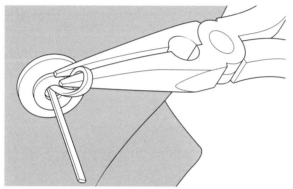

Insert the plastic joint through the gap in the arm left for stuffing and into the hole made in the arm for the joint (as marked on paper patterns).

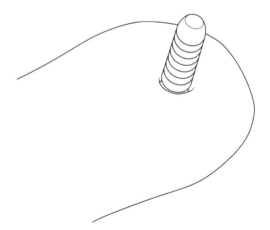

Stuff around the joint and then stitch up the stuffing gap using ladder stitch.

Push the joint (now attached to the arm) through the hole made in the body for arm placement, from the outside in. On the inside push on the plastic washer and then firmly push on the plastic locking washer.

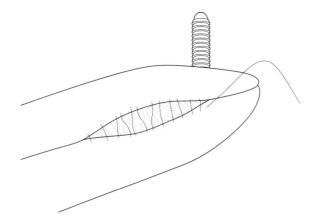

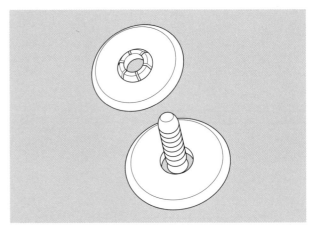

Always check you have the arm in the right position before attaching the locking washer. It cannot be removed once locked in place without destroying it.

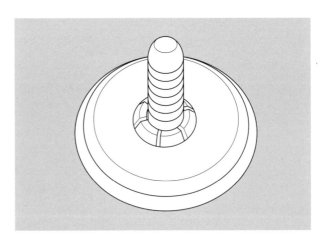

FACES

EYES

When making up the eyes, you will need to cut a card shape and make the central hole where marked. Then, using the card as a guide, cut two pieces of 2oz wadding and felt 1cm (⅜in) bigger all around than the card pattern. You will then have a plastic safety eye and washer back, an iris (note: not all characters have an iris), and card, wadding and felt circles.

Push the safety eye through the iris then through the card-and-felt eye piece, then push the eye through the hole made on the body/head piece for the eye placement from the outside in. On the inside secure with the metal washer (some safety eyes have plastic washers but it works the same way).

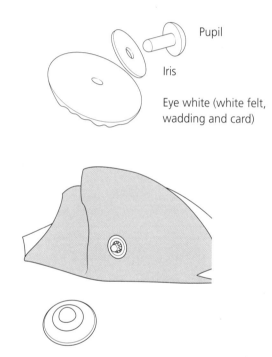

Pupil

Iris

Eye white (white felt, wadding and card)

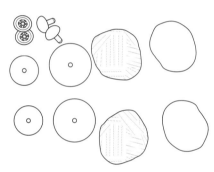

Using running stitch, gather up the felt to fit tightly around the card and wadding pieces and secure. From the back push a bradawl through the hole in the cardboard and then through the wadding and felt.

MOUTHS

Most of the mouths are made up of a black mouth shape with white teeth slip stitched on top (some have an upper and lower set of teeth). Slip stitch around the teeth shape onto the black mouth piece, then stitch in position on the face along the top and bottom edge of the teeth and mouth.

THE CREATURES

LOTTIE OXYL

HEIGHT: 71CM (28IN)

Semi-aquatic Lottie Oxyl is the underwater music correspondent for respected news website The Gill. Along with her brother Lonnie, she founded the record label POND and helped launch the career of scaly crooner Sam Alander. She enjoys drizzly weather, weak tea and polka dots.

YOU WILL NEED:

FELT
- Yellow, 80 x 50cm (31½ x 20in)
- Black, 20 x 30cm (8 x 11¾in)
- Pink, 6 x 4cm (2⅜ x 1⅝in)
- Grey, 20 x 8cm (8 x 3¼in)
- White, 10 x 8cm (4 x 3¼in)

- Long-pile fake fur, 16 x 16cm (6¼ x 6¼in)
- Pair of 16mm (⅝in) plastic black safety eyes
- 2 x 16mm (⅝in) plastic toy joints
- Polyester fibre stuffing
- Dress fabric (I used polka dot polycotton), 55 x 90cm (22 x 36in)
- Ric-rac braid, 1m 60cm (63in)
- 2cm (¾in) wide ribbon, 55cm (21⅝in)
- 5mm (³⁄₁₆in) wide ribbon, 20cm (8in)
- 3 x buttons, approx 1cm (⅜in)
- 3 x press studs, approx 1cm (⅜in)
- 1 x long adult sock

PATTERN PIECES:

BODY
- Head (cut 2 in yellow felt)
- Arm (cut 2 in yellow felt)
- Fingers (cut 2 in grey felt)
- Leg (cut 2 in yellow felt)
- Foot (cut 4 in yellow felt)
- Upper body (cut 2 in yellow felt)
- Lower body (cut 2 in black felt)
- Eyelashes (cut 2 in black felt)
- Eye white (cut 2 in white felt)
- Eyeliner (cut 2 in pink felt)
- Mouth (cut 1 in black felt)
- Teeth (cut 1 in white felt)
- Hair (cut 1 in fake fur)
- Horn (cut 2 in grey felt)

DRESS
- Bodice back (cut 1 in dress fabric)
- Bodice front (cut 2 in dress fabric)
- Collar (cut 2 on bias in dress fabric)
- Sleeve (cut 2 in dress fabric)
- Skirt (no pattern piece, cut a rectangle 90 x 20cm / 35⅜ x 8in)

01. Cut out all pieces in their corresponding fabrics and make holes for arms and eyes with a bradawl. Use a craft knife to cut the slit in the eyelash piece.

02. Stitch the head darts on both pieces then place the two pieces right sides together and stitch all around the head, remembering to leave the gap for stuffing as marked on the pattern. Turn to the right side.

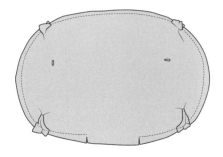

03. Attach the eyes to the body. First insert the white of the eye into the slit made in the eyelash piece, then push the plastic eye through the hole in the eye and eyelash and then into the body where indicated on the pattern, securing with the washer at the back. Slip stitch the eyeliner onto the eye along the top edge. Then slip stitch around the bottom part of the eye onto the body, leaving the eyelashes unstitched. Stuff the head.

04. Slip stitch the teeth to the mouth, then slip stitch the mouth onto the head.

05. Fold each arm lengthwise and insert a finger piece into the bottom straight edge, pointing inward. Stitch across to hold the fingers in place and then along the side and round the bottom, leaving a gap for turning. Turn to the right side. Insert a plastic joint in each arm and stuff.

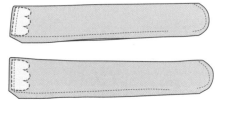

06. Fold each leg lengthways and stitch down the longest edge. Turn to the right side and stuff. Sew running stitch along the top edge of each leg and pull tight to close, securing the thread with small stitches. Repeat with the bottom edges of the legs.

07 Sew the foot pieces together to make a pair of feet. Trim excess fabric from around the stitching and nick in between the toes.

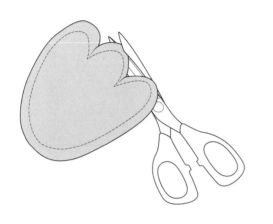

08 Turn to the right side through the cross cut, as marked on the pattern. Stuff lightly.

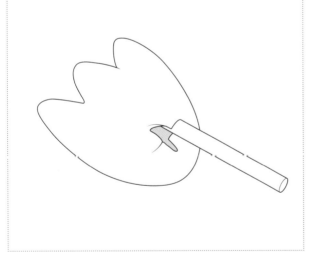

09 Using ladder stitch, attach the feet to the legs. The legs should cover neatly the cross cut in the feet, and the leg seams should be at the back.

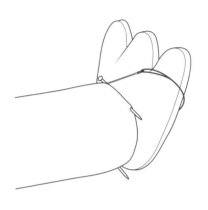

10 Sew the darts in the lower body pieces. With right sides together, stitch each lower body piece to an upper body piece, then place right sides together and stitch down the sides of the upper body piece and around the lower body. Turn to the right side.

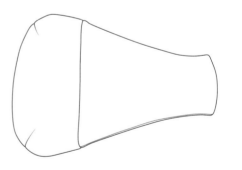

11 Attach the arms to the body with the plastic joints (see page 13), making sure the seams on the arms are at the back. Using ladder stitch, close the gap left for stuffing the arms.

12 Stuff the body. Sew a line of running stitches around the neck edge and pull the raw edge in a little, but not tightly.

13 Pin the head to the body and attach with ladder stitch. Do the same with the legs.

14 Stitch the horn shapes together to make a pair of horns, turn to the right side and stuff. Sew a line of running stitches around the open edge and pull tightly together. Attach to the head with ladder stitch, just below the head dart.

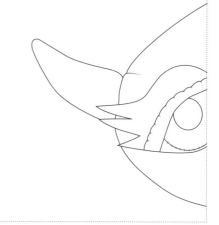

15 Fold in the edges of the fur at the narrow end to meet at the centre. Oversew this edge onto the back of the head, diagonally on the seam but just slightly off centre. Flip the hair over to the front and tack into position. If needed, trim the fur fibres with upward cuts. Never cut straight across the ends, as this will make the hair look too blunt.

LOTTIE'S CLOTHES

01 Using the narrow ribbon, sew a small bow in the centre of the upper and lower body seam to give the impression of underwear.

02 With right sides together, stitch around the outer edge of the collar. Nick around the curves, then turn to the right side and press. Stitch ric-rac braid around the outer edge and press again.

03 Sew together the bodice side seams on either side of the armholes. Press the seams open.

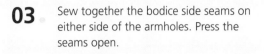
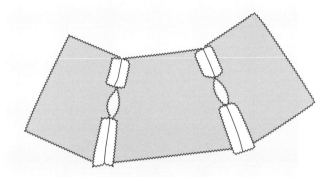

04 Attach the collar to the bodice, folding the centre front facing over the collar as you stitch. Topstitch this seam from the right side to keep the collar facing downwards.

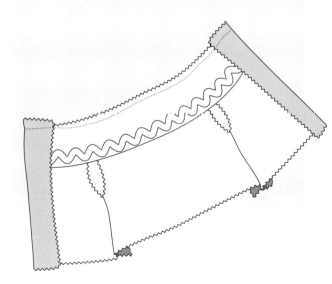

05 Hem the bottom sleeve edges, then trim with ric-rac as shown. With right sides together, sew the underarm seam and press. Drag your nail along the seam to help open it. Turn to the right side.

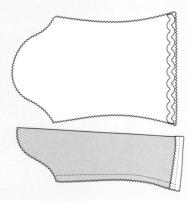

06 Gather the sleeve head between the notches marked on the pattern. Sew two rows of running stitches close together, then pull them up into tight gathers, so the gathered section measures about 1.5cm (⅝in).

07 Matching the underarm seams, and with right sides together, insert and stitch the sleeve into the armhole. This is quite fiddly. If you find it tricky on the machine, hand sew using a small back stitch.

08 Make the skirt. With right sides together, join the short edges, leaving 6cm (2⅜in) from the top unstitched – this will be the centre front. Pin or notch the point opposite the seam at the top of the skirt. This will mark the centre back and help you get the gathers even when attaching the bodice. Sew two rows of running stitch along the top edge, pulling the threads to gather so the skirt fits the bottom edge of the bodice.

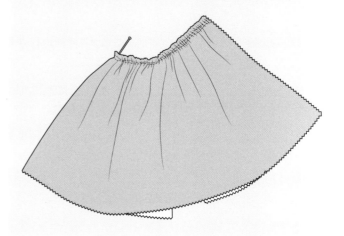

09 Attach the skirt to the bodice, matching notches, folding the front bodice facings over the skirt as you stitch. Hem the skirt and add ric-rac braid to the bottom, with the join at the back.

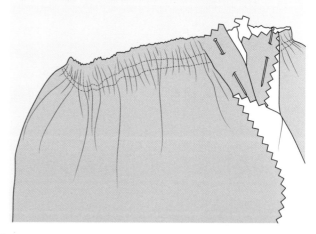

10 Attach buttons and press studs to the centre front opening.

11 From the wider ribbon, cut two pieces 12cm (4¾in) long, each with a diagonal edge at one end. Cut another short piece, about 8cm (3⅛in). Take the remainder, which should be about 23cm (9in), and fold the ends to the centre to make a bow, overlapping by 1cm (⅜in). Sew in place. Wrap the short piece of ribbon around the centre and secure at the back to make the bow knot. Attach the two 12cm (4¾in) pieces to the back of the bow as tails and stitch to the front of the dress.

12 To make the legwarmers, take your sock and cut the top away from the foot, giving you a tube approx 20cm (8in) long. Cut this piece into two pieces lengthways. Fold each piece in half and zigzag the long edge to make a legwarmer. Turn to the right side and pull onto Lottie's legs, tucking the raw bottom edge in.

ROKPOK

ROKPOK

HEIGHT: 70CM (27½IN)

Rokpok's aim in life is to bring joy to people, whether they want it or not. He is always preceded by the distant sound of disco and the faint smell of peardrops. He appears whenever the mood is low and his services are required. His greatest achievements include getting a roomful of tax inspectors to form a gigantic conga line.

YOU WILL NEED:

FELT
- Pink, 85 x 65cm (33½ x 25⅝in)
- Orange, 30 x 30cm (11¾ x 11¾in)
- Purple, 20 x 30cm (8 x 11¾in)
- Black, 10 x 5cm (4 x 2in)
- White, 6 x 4cm (2⅜ x 1⅝in)

- Pair of 16mm (⅝in) black plastic safety eyes
- 2 x 16mm (⅝in) plastic toy joints
- Small piece of cardboard (cereal box is perfect)
- Small piece of 2oz wadding, approx 5 x 10cm (2 x 4in)
- Polyester fibre stuffing

PATTERN PIECES:

- Body (cut 2 in pink felt)
- Arm (cut 4 in pink felt)
- Leg (cut 2 in pink felt)
- Foot (cut 4 in pink felt)
- Beard frill 1 (cut 1 in orange felt)
- Beard frill 2 (cut 1 in pink felt)
- Beard frill 3/eye frill 1 (cut 3 in purple felt, 1 for the beard and 2 for the eyes)
- Eye frill 2 (cut 2 in pink felt)
- Mouth (cut 1 in black felt)
- Upper teeth (cut 1 in white felt)
- Lower teeth (cut 1 in white felt)
- Wrist frill (cut 2 in orange felt)
- Wrist frill appliqué (cut 2 in purple felt)
- Eye (cut 2 in card and 2 slightly bigger in orange felt)
- Neck frill 1 (cut 1 in orange felt)
- Neck frill 2 (cut 1 in purple felt)
- Base (cut 1 in card and 1 slightly bigger in pink felt)
- Nails (cut 2 of each size in orange felt as marked on foot and hand paper pattern)

01. Cut out all the pattern pieces in their corresponding fabrics, making holes for eyes/arms with a bradawl where indicated. (See page 10 for tips on cutting out.)

02. Fold the arms in half lengthwise and stitch down and around the fingers, paying attention to the stitch lines and gaps marked on the pattern. Leave the top edge open. Carefully nick in between the fingers, turn to the right side and stuff. Attach a plastic joint to the top of the arm (see page 13). Close the gap at the wrist using ladder stitch and sew on the fingernails with slip stitch.

03. Fold the legs in half lengthwise and stitch along the long edge. Turn to the right side and stuff. Sew running stitch around the top edge of each leg and pull tight to close, securing the thread with a few stitches. Repeat on the bottom edge of each leg.

04. Sew the foot pieces together, making sure you have a pair of feet, then trim excess fabric close to the stitching and nick in between the toes. Turn to the right side through the cross cut and stuff lightly. See Lottie Oxyl, step 7 on page 21.

05. Attach the feet to the legs using ladder stitch. Make sure the leg seams are at the back and the cross cut is hidden by the end of the leg. Sew on the toenails using slip stitch. See Lottie Oxyl, step 9 on page 21.

06. Make up the eyes (see page 15). Pin the eye frills (two layers) to the back of each eye and stitch in place along the top edge of the eye, making sure you catch both layers. Attach the eyes to the front body using a washer on the reverse.

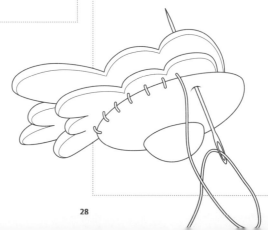

07. Sew the darts in the body shapes, then put them right sides together and stitch around the outer edge, leaving the bottom open for stuffing. Take care not to catch the eye frills when sewing; you may need to tuck them out of the way. Turn the body to the right side.

09. Place the card base onto the felt base. Sew running stitch around the edges and draw the felt up to fit neatly over the card.

08. Attach the arms to the body using a plastic washer (see page 13) and then stuff the body.

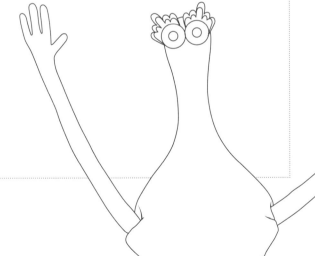

10. With a running stitch, gather up the bottom of the body just enough to draw the raw edge in a bit. Pin the base to the bottom and hand stitch in place. Attach the legs to the body using ladder stitch.

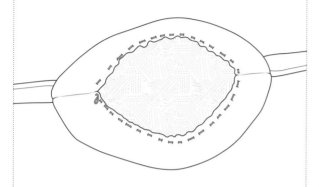

12. Wrap the first neck frill around the neck and stitch the edges together to secure. Repeat with the second frill.

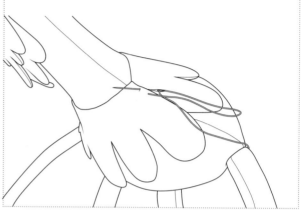

11. Layer all three beard frills on top of each other and oversew onto the face, making sure you catch all the layers. Slip stitch the teeth to the mouth, then slip stitch the mouth to the face, so it covers where you attached the beard frills.

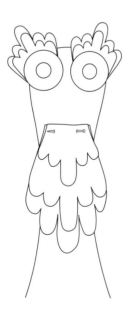

13. Slip stitch the appliqué detail onto the wrist frills, then secure the frills to the wrists by stitching the edges together.

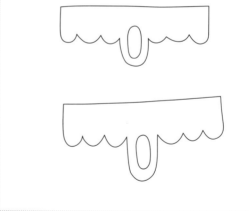

BIRD WRANGLER

BIRD WRANGLER

HEIGHT: 82CM (32¼IN)

Since birth the Bird Wrangler has had an affinity with all avian life. He knew if anyone could wrangle birds, then he could! Other members of his family have specialized their wrangling businesses to specific birds, but the Bird Wrangler's motto is 'Come one, come all'. He's currently out there now wrangling like his life depends on it.

YOU WILL NEED:

FELT
- Pale aqua, 95 x 50cm (37½ x 20in)
- Aqua, 20 x 30cm (8 x 11¾in)
- White, 15 x 20cm (6 x 8in)
- Black, 10 x 5cm (4 x 2in)

- Medium-pile aqua fake fur, 55 x 32cm (21⅝ x 12⅝in)
- Small pieces of card (cereal box is perfect)
- 2oz thick wadding, approx 12 x 12cm (4¾ x 4¾in)
- 1 x 16mm (⅝in) black plastic safety eye
- Polyester fibre stuffing

PATTERN PIECES:

- Body (cut 2 in pale aqua felt)
- Lower leg (cut 2 in fake fur)
- Upper leg (cut 2 in pale aqua felt)
- Lower arm (cut 2 in fake fur)
- Upper arm (cut 2 in pale aqua felt)
- Horn (cut 4 in aqua felt)
- Base (cut 1 in pale aqua felt)
- Outer beard (cut 1 in fake fur)
- Inner beard (cut 1 in pale aqua felt)
- Mouth (cut 1 in black felt)
- Upper teeth (cut 1 in white felt)
- Lower teeth (cut 1 in white felt)
- Eye (cut 1 in card and 2 slightly bigger in white felt)
- Eye iris (cut 1 in aqua felt)

01. Cut out all the pattern pieces in their corresponding fabrics. See page 10 for tips on cutting out.

02. Stitch the darts on the front and back body pieces.

03. Make up the eye (see page 15) and attach to the body front where indicated on the pattern.

04. With right sides together, join the bottom fur piece to the top felt piece on all four limbs. Fold the limbs lengthwise, right sides together, and stitch down the longest edge, opening the seam that joins the fur to the felt as you sew. With the edge of your scissors tuck any stray fur fibres into the bottom edge and sew across to close. Turn to the right side and, using a pin or a wire teazel brush, pick any trapped fur fibres out of the bottom seam. Then stuff all four limbs.

05. On the back body piece and the base piece, machine stitch along the gap marked for the stuffing opening. This will stop the felt stretching when you stuff later.

07. Put the body pieces right sides together with the legs and arms tucked up between them. Stitch together around the outer edge, leaving the bottom edge open where indicated on the pattern.

08. Pin the base to the body pieces, then stitch together, remembering to leave the gap for stuffing. This stage is quite tricky so you may find it easier to hand stitch the pieces first.

06. Pin the legs and arms into position onto the front body, as marked on the pattern, with seams facing inwards. Stitch to hold in place.

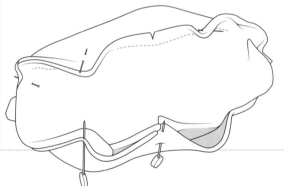

09. Turn to the right side, pulling the legs through first. Stuff the body, then close the gap with ladder stitch.

10. Stitch the darts in the outer beard piece, then pin to the inner beard piece with right sides together. Stitch, and then turn to the right side. Stuff lightly, then stitch the gap closed.

11. Stitch the white teeth to the black mouth piece, then stitch the mouth to the beard where indicated on the pattern.

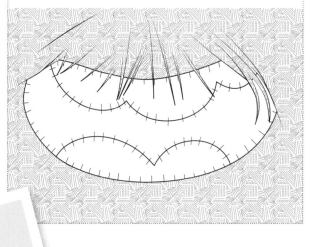

12. Pin the beard into position on the body, and hand sew in place using a wide ladder stitch, stitching only through the felt section of the beard. The stitches should be easily hidden in the pile of the fur along the beard edge.

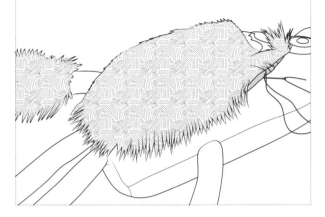

13. Stitch the horn pieces together to make two horns, turn to the right side and stuff. Sew running stitch around the outer edge of the horns and pull the stitches tight to close the gap. Secure the thread with small stitches. Using ladder stitch, attach the horns to the body, near where the darts are and the head starts to curve.

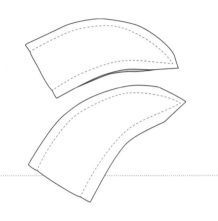

MYRTLE SNOOKS

HEIGHT: 70CM (27½IN)

Myrtle is the best-selling author of a series of novels about a French vet turned detective, set in Utrecht in the 1930s. Despite literary success she's almost as famous for her fondness for horse racing, tweed and sherry, and in 2009 was named Tweed Wearer of the Year by the Society for Slightly Itchy Fabrics.

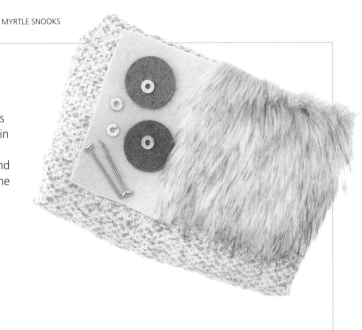

YOU WILL NEED:

FELT
- Pale grey, 25 x 45cm (10 x 17¾in) in a colour to match the fur (see below)
- Blue, 20 x 20cm (8 x 8in)
- White, 15 x 18cm (6 x 7¼in)

- Medium-pile grey fake fur, approx 70 x 50cm (27½ x 20in)
- Small pieces of card (cereal box is perfect)
- Small piece of 2oz thick wadding, approx 10 x 15cm (4 x 6in)
- Pair of 16mm (⅝in) black plastic safety eyes
- 2 x cotter pin joints, approx 15mm (⅝in)
- Polyester stuffing
- Material for the cape (I used wool tweed), 1m (1 yard)
- Lining fabric, 60cm (23⅝in)
- 6 x buttons, approx 30mm (1⅛in)
- 3 x press studs (snaps), approx 10mm (⅜in)

PATTERN PIECES:

BODY
- Body (cut 2 in fake fur)
- Lower limb (cut 4 in fake fur)
- Upper limb (cut 4 in pale grey felt)
- Horn (cut 2 in blue felt)
- Eye (cut 2 in card and 2 slightly bigger in white felt)
- Eye iris (cut 2 in blue felt)

CAPE
- Cape front (cut 2 in cape fabric and 2 in lining)
- Cape back (cut 1 on fold in cape fabric and 1 on fold in lining)
- Jet (cut 4 in cape fabric)
- Collar (cut 1 on fold in cape fabric)

01. Cut out all the pattern pieces in their corresponding fabrics. (See page 10 for tips on cutting out.)

02. Stitch the darts on the body shapes, tucking in any stray fibres with the edge of your scissors as you sew.

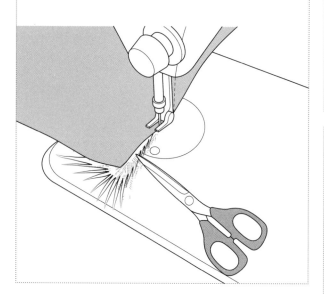

03. Make up the eyes and attach to the body front (see page 15).

04. With right sides together, join the bottom fur piece to the top felt piece on all four limbs. Fold each limb in half lengthwise and sew the long edges together, opening the seam that joins the fur to the felt as you go. With the edge of your scissors tuck any stray fur fibres into the bottom edge and sew across to close. Turn to the right side and, using a pin or teazel brush, pick any trapped fur fibres out of the bottom seam. Then stuff all four limbs.

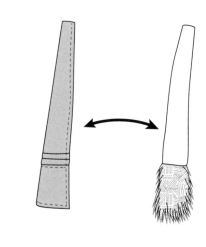

05. Pin the legs into position onto the bottom edge of the front body, with seams facing inwards. Stitch in place.

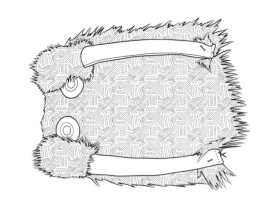

06. Place the body pieces right sides together and, with the legs tucked inside out of the way, stitch around the outer edge, remembering to leave a gap for stuffing. I find it easiest to start at the top and go down one side, turn over and then from the same start position stitch down the other side. This way you are always stitching in the direction of the fur pile, which is so much easier. Turn to the right side.

07. Attach the arms to the body with cotter pin joints (see page 12).

08. Stuff the body and then sew up the gap with ladder stitch.

09. Fold the felt horn pieces in half and stitch along the longest edge, turn to the right side and stuff. Sew running stitch around the open end of the horn and pull the stitches tight to close the gap. Secure the thread with small stitches. Using ladder stitch, attach the horns to the body, near where the darts are and the head starts to curve.

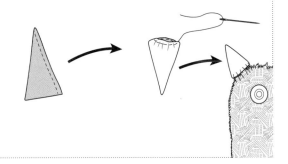

10. Release any fur fibres caught in the body seams with a pin or teazel brush.

MYRTLE'S CLOTHES

03. On the right side of each front piece, place two jets with raw edges together along the stitched line. Stitch in the centre of each of the strips to the exact length of the original positioning line. It is important that all three stitched lines are exactly the same length; check this on the reverse.

01. On the reverse of the front pieces, mark the arm slit positions with tailor's chalk or pencil, then stitch along this line so that the positioning is visible from the right side.

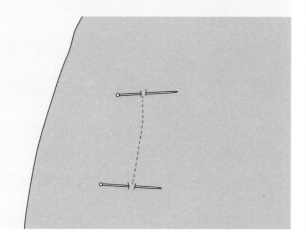

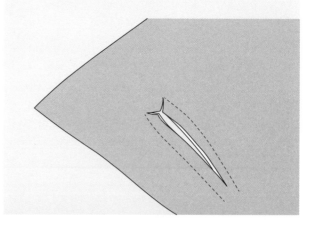

02. Fold all the jets for the armholes in half lengthwise with wrong sides together. Stitch together close to the longest edge.

04. From the reverse side, trim along the central stitched line to approx 1cm (⅜in) from each end of the stitching. Cut a V-shaped slit from this central line to each of the outer stitched lines.

05. Turn the strips to the right side and, from the reverse, stitch across the ends of the strips and the V cut.

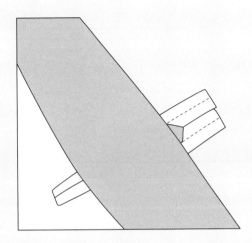

07. With wrong sides together, fold the collar in half and stitch down the two ends, turn to the right side and pin along the bottom edge. Stitch this edge to hold in position.

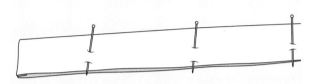

06. With right sides together, sew the side seams of the cape, joining fronts to back. Do the same with the lining. Press the seams open on the cape and the lining.

08. Pin the collar to the top edge of the cape and stitch in place.

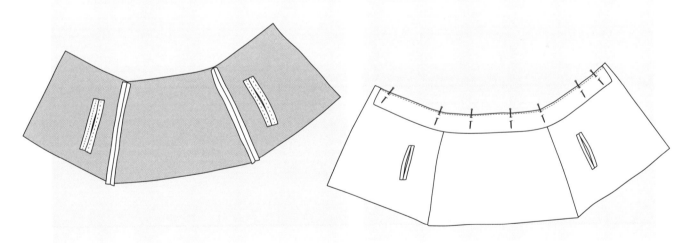

09. Pin the lining to the cape, right sides together, and stitch along the front edges and hem. Topstitch along this seam on the lining side.

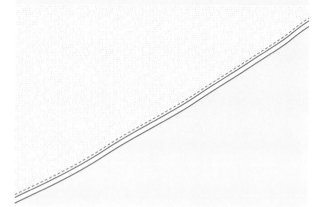

10. Pin the top edge of the lining to the collar seam and stitch together, leaving a gap in the centre to turn out. Turn to the right side, press and hand sew the gap.

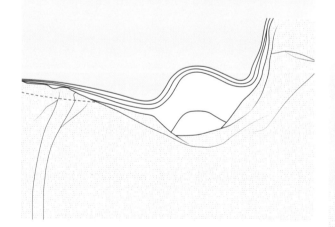

11. Pin the lining to the armhole strips and cut along the centre, making a V cut at each end. Turn the raw edges inwards and hand sew in place.

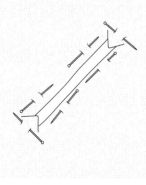

12. Sew the buttons to the right side of the cape.

13. Fit the cape on Myrtle and mark positions for the press studs with pins. Sew on three press studs. The collar should fit snugly to prevent slipping.

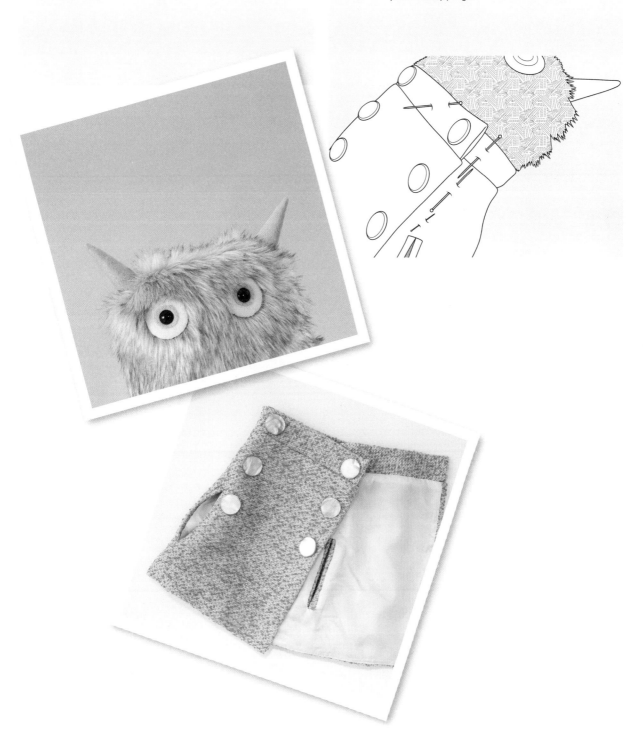

Beardo

Hand puppet designed by Pete Fowler

BEARDO HAND PUPPET
DESIGNED BY PETE FOWLER

HEIGHT: 32CM (80IN)

Meet Beardo! Sporting one of the finest facial growths this side of the universe, he has many inhabitants in his beard: a family of field mice, two barn owls, a stoat and a spider monkey that escaped from the local zoo. When he's not grooming his beard, he likes to dig around in charity shops, fly owls and do puzzle magazines in his garden.

YOU WILL NEED:

FELT
- Cream, 40 x 50cm (16 x 20in)
- Brown, 40 x 40cm (16 x 16in)
- Dark brown, 25 x 20cm (10 x 8in)
- Pink, 18 x 20cm (7¼ x 8in)
- Dark blue, 20 x 25cm (8 x 10in)
- Light blue, 15 x 10cm (6 x 4in)
- Orange, 26 x 15cm (10¼ x 6in)
- Yellow, 26 x 15cm (10¼ x 6in)
- Black, 10 x 3cm (4 x 1¼in)

PATTERN PIECES:

- Body (cut 2 in cream felt)
- Arm (cut 4 in cream felt)
- Nose (cut 2 in pink felt)
- Ear (cut 4 in cream felt)
- Back hair (cut 1 in brown felt)
- Front hair (cut 1 in brown felt)
- Beard (cut 1 in brown felt)
- Moustache (cut 1 in dark brown felt)
- Chin (cut 1 in cream felt)
- Boot (cut 4 in brown felt)
- Turn-up (cut 4 in light blue felt)
- Leg (cut 4 in dark blue felt)
- Letter B (cut 1 in dark blue felt)
- Sleeve 1 (cut 4 in orange felt)
- Sleeve 2 (cut 4 in yellow felt)
- Jeans (cut 2 in dark blue felt)
- Jumper stripe
  (cut 4 in orange felt and 4 in yellow felt)
- Eye (cut 2 in black felt)

01. Cut out all the pattern pieces in their corresponding fabrics.

02. Pin the back hair piece onto one of the body pieces and slip stitch together along the bottom edge of the hair. Attach the jeans to the bottom of the body piece in the same way.

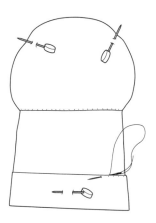

03. Do the same with the front hair (slip stitching the inside edge of the hairline) and the jeans on the other body piece.

04. Pin the jumper stripes onto the body in alternating colours, overlapping them slightly, and then slip stitch along the longest edges to keep them in place. Do the same with both body pieces, carefully checking that the stripes match up on both of them.

05. Attach the sleeve stripes to the arms in the same way, making sure you sew all the pieces to make up two pairs of arms.

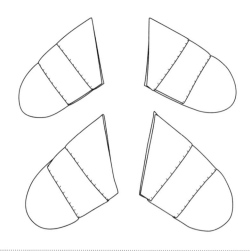

06. With right sides together, pin a pair of arms to each body piece between notches (see pattern markings) and sew the seam, either on the sewing machine or with a small back stitch. Make a neat nick into the seam above and below the arm so you can open the seam out.

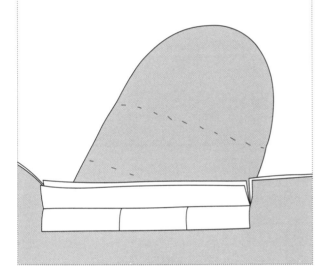

07. Sew together the boots, turn-ups and leg pieces, again making sure you sew all the pieces to make up two pairs of legs. Then, with right sides together, sew two pieces together to make a leg, opening the seams as you stitch over them. Repeat to make the second leg.

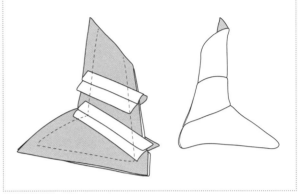

08. Turn the legs to the right side and pin in place on either side of the front body piece.

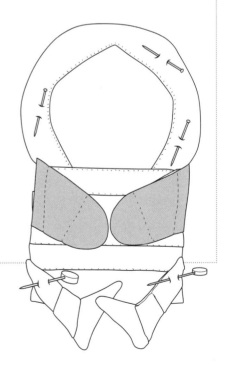

09. Make up two ears by putting pairs of pieces right sides together and stitching around the curved edge. Turn to the right side and pin onto the head, following the pattern piece for placement.

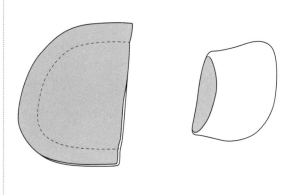

11. Make up the nose by stitching the two pieces with right sides together all around the outside edge. Turn to the right side through the slit made in the back. Stuff lightly.

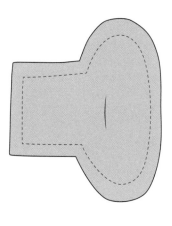

10. Pin both body pieces right sides together and stitch all around, changing thread colour as the felt colour changes, and leaving the bottom edge open. Turn to the right side.

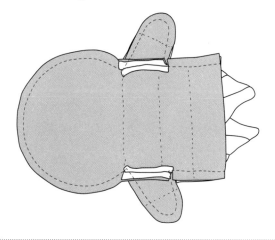

12. Slip stitch the chin to the front body piece.

13. Slip stitch the beard just under the chin, only stitching along the top curved edge.

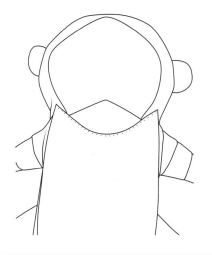

15. Slip stitch the eyes and moustache into position on the face. If the moustache flops around too much, put some small stitches on the ends to secure it.

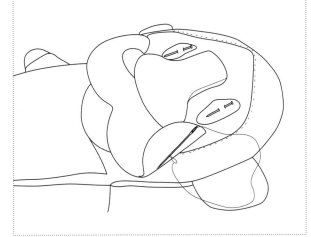

14. Slip stitch the moustache onto the face (you only need to secure the central section). Then ladder stitch the nose in place, with the slit side facing down.

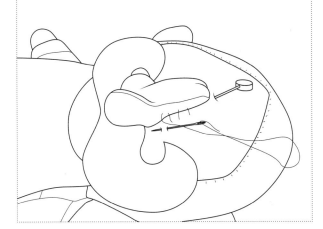

16. Finally, slip stitch the B onto Beardo's back. Then slip your hand in and say hello to puppet Beardo!

CORNEY ISLAND DAWG
DESIGNED BY JON BURGERMAN

HEIGHT: 46CM (18¼IN)

Corney Island Dawg is a member of a renegade band of do-gooder wieners. They escaped the indignity of being eaten for sport at the annual Corney Island Hot Dawg Eating Contest. If you're in a pickle – or if you are a pickle – they will find a way to help you.

YOU WILL NEED:

FELT
- Brown, 30 x 35cm (12 x 14in)
- Yellow, 25 x 60cm (10 x 23⅝in)
- Red, 40 x 26cm (16 x 10¼in)
- Orange, 15 x 20cm (6 x 8in)
- Mustard, 15 x 3cm (6 x 1¼in)
- Small piece of black for mouth
- White, 15 x 10cm (6 x 4in)

- 6oz wadding, 25 x 30cm (10 x 12in)
- Small pieces of cardboard (cereal box is perfect)
- Pair of 10mm (⅜in) plastic oval safety eyes
- Sequins in red and mustard yellow (approx 2g of each)
- Polyester fibre stuffing
- Small piece of brown embroidery thread
- 12mm (½in) button (any colour, as it will be covered in felt)

PATTERN PIECES:

- Jacket (cut 4 in yellow felt)
- Wadding (cut 2 in 6oz wadding)
- Body (cut 1 in brown felt)
- Arm (cut 2 in brown felt)
- Boot (cut 4 in red felt)
- Sock (cut 4 in white felt)
- Leg (cut 4 in brown felt)
- Sole (cut 2 in red felt)
- Cap (cut 2 in orange felt and 2 in red felt)
- Peak (cut 2 in orange felt)
- Mouth (cut 1 in black felt)
- Teeth (cut 1 in white felt)
- Eye (cut 2 in card and 2 slightly bigger in white felt)
- Ketchup (cut 1 in red felt)
- Mustard (cut 1 in mustard felt)
- Scarf (cut 1 in red felt on fold)

01. Cut out all pattern pieces in their corresponding fabrics, remembering to cut holes in the wadding and circular cuts in the jacket pieces for armholes.

02. Make up and attach the eyes (see page 15).

03. Stitch the teeth to the back of the black mouth piece (this is a bit fiddly), then stitch the mouth to the body.

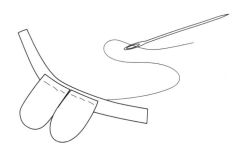

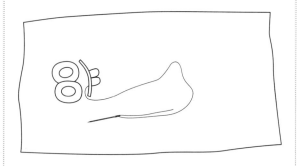

04. With right sides together, fold the body piece and stitch along the longest edge, then turn to the right side and stuff.

05. At the top and bottom of the body piece, turn in the raw edges and run a row of running stitches at the folded edge. Pull these stitches tight to close the gap and then secure the thread.

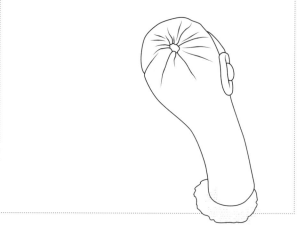

06. Fold the arms, right sides together, and stitch along the longest edge and around the bottom edge. Turn to the right side and stuff.

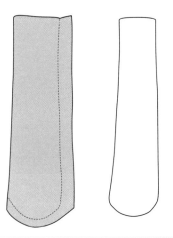

08. Stitch the arms with ladder stitch to the body, checking the pattern pieces for placement.

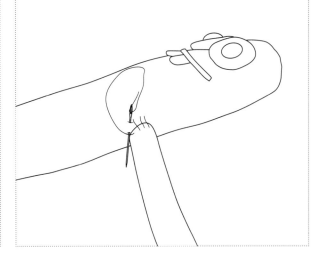

07. With embroidery thread, sew long stitches over the bottom edges of the arms, pulling the stitches tight to form finger shapes. At the other open end of the arm, draw up the raw edge with running stitches, pulling tight to close the gap.

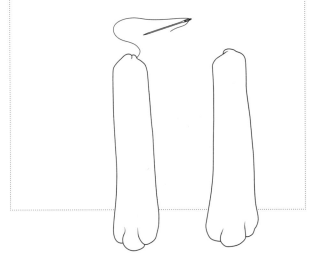

09. Join together the boots, socks and legs, making sure you sew all the pieces to make up two pairs of legs. With right sides together stitch a pair of leg pieces along the front and back edges, opening the seams as you stitch over them. Pin the sole into the bottom edge of the boot/leg and stitch in place. Turn to the right side and stuff the legs/boots. Make up the second leg/boot in the same way.

10. Cut a strip of white felt 5mm (¼in) wide and long enough to go around the bottom edge of the boots, and slip stitch in place. Cut two small strips of red felt, wrap around the top edge of the boot and stitch in place to neaten the seam where the sock joins the boot. Finally, cut eight small strips of white felt and stitch four to each boot to represent laces.

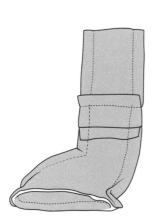

11. Attach the legs to the body with ladder stitch.

12. Sew matching sequins onto the mustard and ketchup felt shapes. It's easier if you stitch sequins all around the edges first then fill in the centre. Overlap the sequins as you stitch, stitching back through the hole of the previous sequin each time. Stitch the completed sequinned pieces to the body, using the photo as a guide for position.

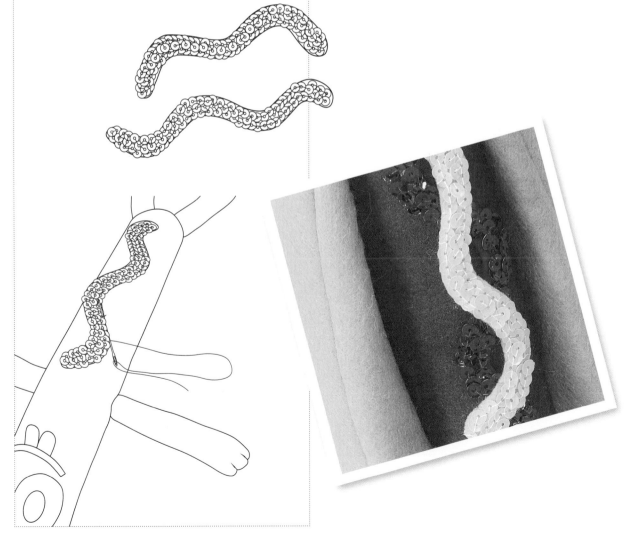

13. Pin the wadding to two of the jacket pieces (the other two pieces are the jacket lining). With right sides together, stitch down the straight edge to join the two outer (wadded) jacket pieces. Repeat with the lining jacket pieces but remember to leave the small gap as marked on the pattern piece. Open the pieces out.

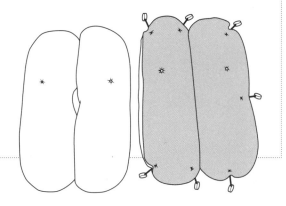

14. With right sides together, stitch all around the edges of the outer and lining jacket pieces. Trim the wadding bulk carefully from around the curved edges of this seam. Nick into the seam at the centre back, top and bottom, then turn to the right side.

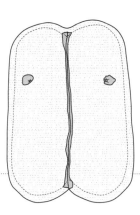

15. Sew around the armholes in the jacket using small stitches and pushing the raw edges in on both the lining and the outer edge. This is a bit tricky, but persevere.

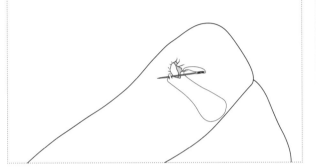

17. Tie the scarf around the neck of your Corney Island Dawg. Put his jacket on and tack it to the body with a few ladder stitches near the armholes and bottom edge to keep it in place. Put on his hat and he's ready to go!

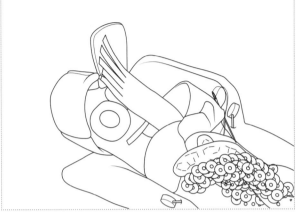

16. Sew all four cap pieces together, alternating the colours. Turn to the right side. Place the two peak pieces together and sew around the curved edge, then turn to the right side. Pin the peak to the edge of the cap and stitch in place. Turn under the raw edge of the cap and sew in place. Cut a piece of felt slightly bigger than the button and gather up with running stitch, pulling tight around the button. Stitch this to the top of the cap.

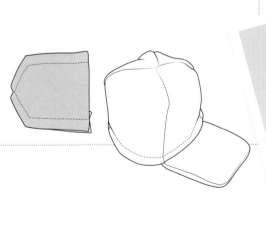

FRINGLE

HEIGHT SEATED: 26CM (10¼IN)
(WITH LEGS OUTSTRETCHED 55CM/22IN)

Fringle is a forest-dwelling collector of 'snazzy' socks
and legwarmers. A renowned dancer, Fringle is capable
of such difficult moves as 'The Toadstool Boogie', 'The
Custard Cream' and 'The Leaf Blower's Cha-Cha-Cha'.
If you're lucky you can spot Fringle on frosty mornings
in January teaching badgers to moonwalk.

YOU WILL NEED:

FELT
- Aqua, 70 x 30cm (27½ x 12in)
- White, 20 x 8cm (8 x 3¼in)
- Black, 6 x 6cm (2⅜ x 2⅜in)

- Long-pile white fake fur, 80 x 30cm (32 x 12in)
- One sock
- 2oz wadding, 5 x 5cm (2 x 2in)
- Pair of 18mm (¾in) black plastic eyes
- 2 x 15mm (⅝in) plastic or cotter pin joints
- Polyester fibre stuffing
- Small pieces of cardboard (cereal box is perfect)

PATTERN PIECES:

- Body (cut 2 in fake fur)
- Body gusset (cut 2 in fake fur)
- Arm (cut 2 in aqua felt)
- Leg (cut 2 in aqua felt)
- Card base (cut 1 in card)
- Felt base (cut 1 in aqua felt)
- Toes (cut 4 in aqua felt)
- Foot pad (cut 2 in aqua felt)
- Eye (cut 2 in card and 2 slightly
  bigger in both white felt and wadding)
- Mouth (cut 1 in black felt)
- Teeth (cut 1 in white felt)

01. Cut out all the pattern pieces in their corresponding fabrics and make holes for the arms and eyes with a bradawl.

02. Make up the eyes (see page 15) and attach to the front body.

03. Match the two gusset pieces right sides together and stitch along the short edge furthest from the armhole, making sure the pile of the fur is going downwards from this seam.

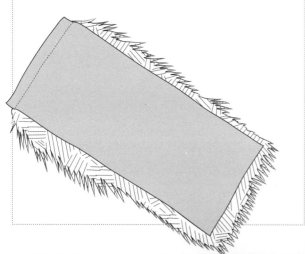

04. With right sides together stitch the gusset round the curve of the front body piece, matching side notches and matching the notch at the top of the body piece with the gusset seam you stitched in 03. Tuck in any stray fur fibres as you sew. Stitch the other edge of the gusset to the back body piece in the same way. It's much easier if you always have the gusset piece on the top as you stitch. Turn to the right side.

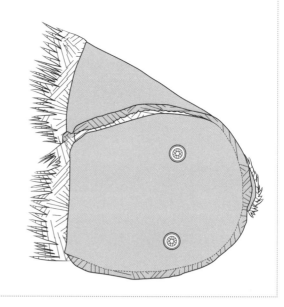

05. Fold each felt arm in half lengthwise and stitch along the longest edge and around the finger curves. Snip into the curves with your scissors, then turn to the right side and stuff. Attach the joints to the ends of the arms (see page 12).

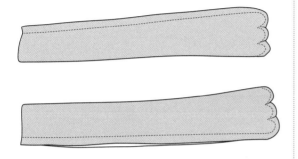

07. Place two toe pieces together and sew around the sides and curved edges. Snip into the curves, then turn to the right side and stuff lightly.

06. Fold each felt leg in half lengthwise and stitch down the longest edge. Pin a circular foot pad to the bottom edge of each foot, matching the quarters, and stitch in place. Turn to the right side and stuff.

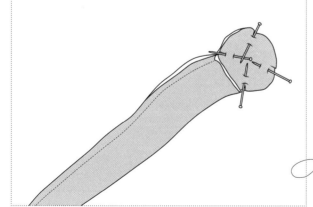

08. Pin a set of toes to the bottom of each leg at the front, tucking in the raw edge of the toe pieces as you sew them in place and making sure the leg seam is at the back.

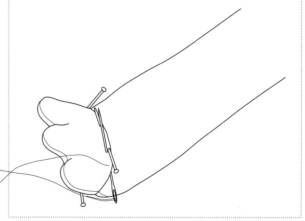

09. Stitch the top edges of the legs in position on the right side of the front of the body.

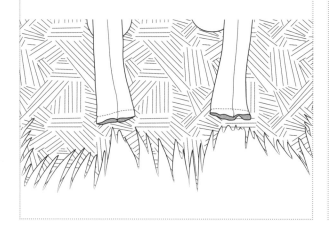

11. Stuff the body and then gather up the raw bottom edge with running stitch. Gather slightly and not too tight.

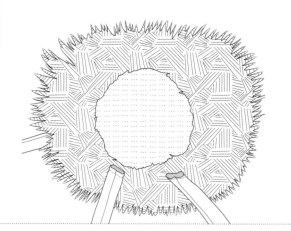

10. Attach the arms to the body gusset on each side using joints (see page 12).

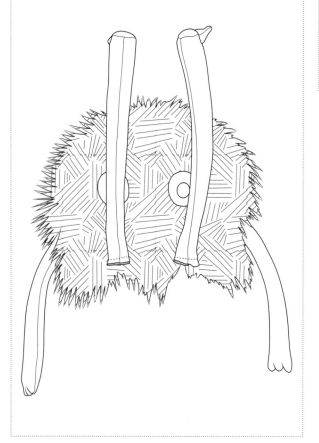

12. Using running stitch, gather along the circumference of the felt base piece until it fits neatly around the card case piece. The eye whites are made the same way.

13. Pin the base onto the bottom of the body, making sure the legs are outside, and matching the quarters. Secure with a ladder stitch.

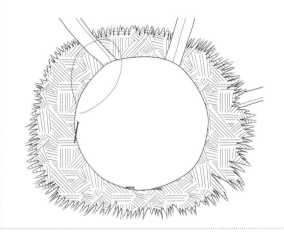

14. Slip stitch the teeth to the mouth, then slip stitch the mouth into position.

15. To make the legwarmers, cut across the sock 20cm (8in) down from the top, then cut this piece into two pieces lengthwise. Fold each piece in half with wrong sides together and zigzag down the edge to form a legwarmer. Turn to the right side and pull onto the leg, tucking the raw bottom edge in once you have arranged on Fringle's leg.

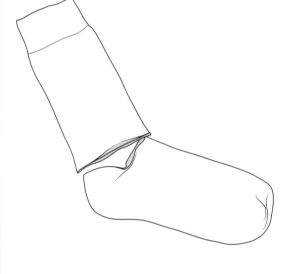

GRUNCH

HEIGHT: 52CM (20¾IN)

Poor old Grunch. He's always wanted to roller-skate but, due to his long furry arms, he can't skate for more than a few minutes without getting tangled up in his own limbs. On the plus side, he's brilliant at wallpapering and is more than happy to be paid in broken chocolate biscuits.

YOU WILL NEED:

FELT
- Orange, 16 x 14cm (6¼ x 5½in)
- Grey, 22 x 35cm (8¾ x 13¾in)
- White, 7 x 14cm (2¾ x 5½in)

- Long-pile grey/white fake fur, 75 x 75cm (30 x 30in)
- 2oz wadding, 7 x 14cm (2¾ x 5½in)
- Pair of 18mm (¾in) plastic black safety eyes
- 2 x 16mm (⅝in) plastic toy joints
- Polyester fibre stuffing
- T-shirt or T-shirt fabric, 75 x 35cm (30 x 14in)
- Iron-on black flock material or black felt, 10 x 8cm (4 x 3⅛in)
- Small pieces of cardboard (cereal box is perfect)

PATTERN PIECES:

- Body (cut 2 in fake fur)
- Arm (cut 2 in fake fur)
- Leg (cut 2 in fake fur)
- Foot pad (cut 2 in orange felt)
- Fingers (cut 2 in orange felt)
- Horn (cut 4 in grey felt)
- Eye (cut 2 in card and 2 slightly bigger in both white felt and wadding)
- Nose (cut 2 in grey felt)
- T-shirt (cut 2 in old T-shirt/stretch fabric)
- Sleeve (cut 2 in old T-shirt/stretch fabric)
- Number 6 (cut in iron-on flock fabric or felt)

01. Cut out all the pattern pieces in their corresponding fabrics, and make holes for arms and eyes with a bradawl. Before cutting his T-shirt out, please read the instructions on page 72.

03. Make up the eyes and attach to the body (see page 15). Grunch has no irises, just whites and pupils.

02. Stitch the darts on the body shapes, tucking in any stray fibres as you sew. With right sides together, sew around the two body pieces, leaving a gap at the bottom for stuffing. Turn to the right side.

04. Pushing the fur upwards out of the way, stitch the felt claws onto the bottom edge of the arms.

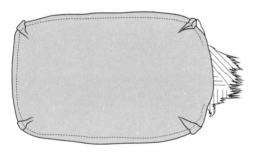

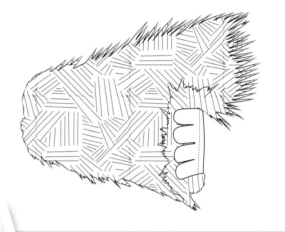

05. Fold each arm in half lengthwise with right sides together and the claws inside. Sew round the edges, remembering to leave the small gap near the top as marked on the pattern. When stitching the bottom edges of the arms, tuck the stray fibres upwards with the edge of your scissors. Turn to the right side and, using a pin or teazel brush, pick out any trapped fur fibres.

06. Stuff the arms, then stitch up the gap left at the top with ladder stitch. Attach to the body with plastic joints (see page 13).

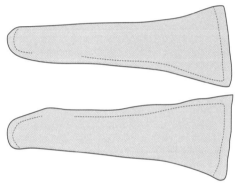

07. Stuff the body and then stitch up the gap left for stuffing using ladder stitch.

08. Stitch the two nose pieces together and turn to the right side through the cross slit in one of the pieces. Lightly stuff and attach to Grunch's face with the slit side down, using ladder stitches around the under edge of the nose.

09. Sew each pair of horn pieces together around the sides and point, leaving the bottom open. Turn to the right side, stuff and then close the gap with a tight running stitch. Attach to the side of the head.

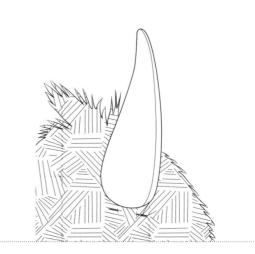

10. Make up the legs by folding each in half lengthwise with right sides together and stitching down the longest edge, tucking in stray fibres as you stitch. Pin a felt foot pad into the wide bottom of each leg, tucking the fur fibres inside and matching the four quarter notches. Sew in place and turn to the right side.

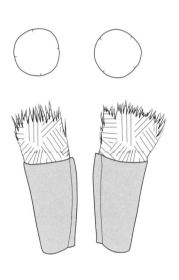

11. Stuff the legs and, using running stitch and strong thread, gather up the stitches to close the top of the leg. Attach the legs to the body using ladder stitch.

GRUNCH'S CLOTHES

01. If you are using an existing T-shirt to make Grunch's T-shirt, lay the front and back pattern pieces along its bottom edge – this will give you a finished edge so there is no need to hem. Do the same with the sleeves. If you are using a piece of T-shirt fabric, add 3cm (1¼in) to the bottom of both patterns and then turn under and hem these edges by hand.

02. With right sides together, join the side seams of the front and back jumper pieces and the underarm seams on the sleeve pieces using a small zigzag machine stitch. Turn the sleeve pieces to the right side.

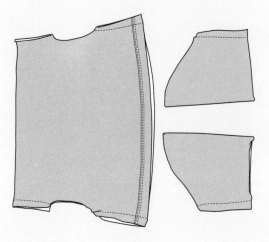

03. With right sides together and matching the underarm seams of the sleeves with the underarms of the body pieces, stitch the sleeves into the armholes using a small zigzag machine stitch. Turn to the right side.

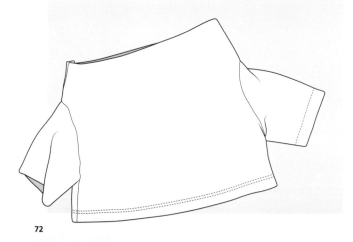

04. Fold down the neckline inside to where marked on the paper pattern and tack in position at the side seams.

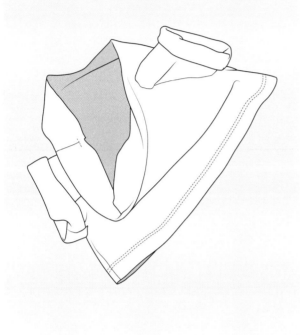

06. Dress Grunch in his T-shirt and double roll up his sleeves, as he prefers them that way.

05. Cut out the number 6 motif in black iron-on flocked fabric and press onto the centre of the T-shirt. Follow the manufacturer's instructions and try out on some scrap fabric first. If you haven't got any iron-on fabric you can cut the motif in felt and hand stitch in place.

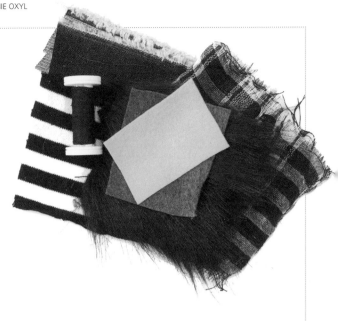

LONNIE OXYL

HEIGHT: 74CM (29½IN)

Lonnie, brother of Lottie, leaves all the important work at POND records to his sister and instead concerns himself more with parties and making sure everyone is having fun. His party-planning book, *Just How Much is Too Much Jelly?*, has topped best-seller lists around the world and his fish-flavoured macarons and pastries are available in subaquatic bakeries nationwide.

YOU WILL NEED:

FELT
- Grey, 95 x 50cm (38 x 20in)
- Black, 12 x 5cm (4¾ x 2in)
- Yellow, 22 x 20cm (8¾ x 8in)
- White, 10 x 11cm (4 x 4⅜in)

- Long-pile black fake fur, 18 x 15cm (7¼ x 6in)
- 2oz wadding, 12 x 6cm (4¾ x 2⅜in)
- Pair of 18mm (¾in) plastic black safety eyes
- 2 x 16mm (⅝in) plastic toy joints
- Polyester fibre stuffing
- Denim, 60 x 40cm (23⅝ x 16in)
- Jumper/T-shirt or knitted jersey fabric, 75 x 25cm (30 x 10in)
- Soft, loosely-woven fabric for scarf, 70 x 70cm (27½ x 27½in)
- Small pieces of cardboard (cereal box is perfect)

PATTERN PIECES:

BODY
- Head (cut 2 in grey felt)
- Leg (cut 2 in grey felt)
- Foot (cut 4 in grey felt)
- Arm (cut 2 in grey felt)
- Fingers (cut 2 in yellow felt)
- Hair (cut 1 in fake fur)
- Horn (cut 4 in yellow felt)
- Upper body (cut 2 in grey felt)
- Lower body (cut 2 in denim)
- Upper teeth (cut 1 in white felt)
- Lower teeth (cut 1 in white felt)
- Mouth (cut 1 in black felt)
- Eye (cut 2 in card and 2 slightly bigger in both white felt and 2oz wadding)
- Iris (cut 2 in yellow felt)

CLOTHES
- Jeans (cut 2 in denim)
- Jumper (cut 2 in old jumper/stretch fabric)
- Jumper sleeve (cut 2 in old jumper/stretch fabric)

01. Cut out all the pattern pieces in their corresponding fabrics and make holes for arms and eyes with a bradawl. Before cutting Lonnie's jumper please read through the instructions on pages 80–83.

04. Slip stitch the teeth to the mouth, then slip stitch the mouth onto the head.

02. Stitch the head darts on both pieces, then place the pieces right sides together and stitch all around the head, leaving a gap for stuffing as marked on the pattern. Turn to the right side.

05. Fold each arm lengthwise and insert a finger piece into the bottom straight edge, pointing inwards. Stitch across to hold the fingers in place and then along the side and round the bottom, leaving a gap for turning. Turn to the right side. Insert a plastic joint in each arm and stuff.

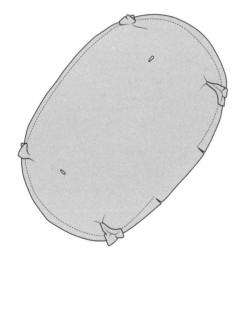

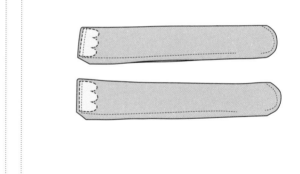

03. Make up the eyes and attach to the head (see page 15). Stuff the head.

06 Fold each leg lengthwise and stitch down the longest edge. Turn to the right side and stuff. Sew running stitch around the top edge of each leg and pull tight to close, securing the thread with small stitches. Repeat with the bottom edges of the legs.

08 Turn to the right side through the cross cut (as marked on pattern). Stuff lightly.

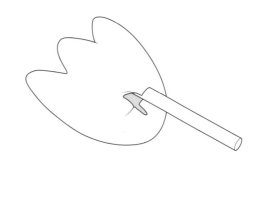

07 Sew the feet pieces together to make a pair of feet. Trim the excess fabric from around the stitching and nick in between the toes.

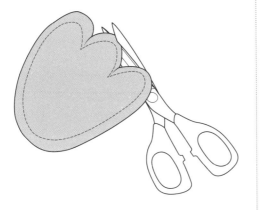

09. Using ladder stitch, attach the feet to the legs. The legs should neatly cover the cross cut in the feet, and the leg seams should be at the back.

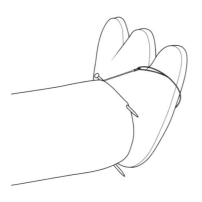

10. Sew the darts in the lower body pieces. With right sides together, stitch each lower body piece to an upper body piece, then place right sides together and stitch down the sides of the upper body piece and around the lower body. Turn to the right side.

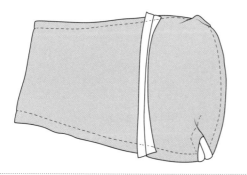

11. Attach the arms to the body with the plastic joints (see page 13), making sure the seams on the arms are at the back. Using ladder stitch, close the gap left for stuffing the arms.

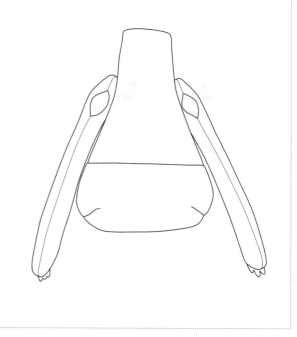

12. Stuff the body. Sew a line of running stitches around the neck edge and pull the raw edge in a little, but not tightly.

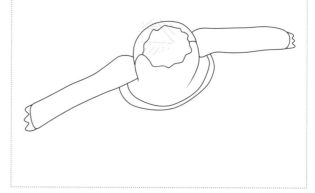

13 Pin the head to the body and attach with ladder stitch.

14 Stitch the horn shapes together to make a pair of horns, turn to the right side and stuff. Sew a line of running stitches around the open edge and pull tightly together. Attach to the head with ladder stitch, just below the head dart.

15 Fold in the edges of the fur at the narrow end to meet at the centre. Oversew this edge onto the back of the head, diagonally on the seam but just slightly off centre. Flip the hair over to the front and tack into position. If needed, trim the fur fibres with upward cuts. Never cut straight across the ends as this will make the hair look too blunt.

LONNIE'S CLOTHES

02 Turn up each jeans leg twice at the bottom to make a nice big 3.5cm (1⅜in) turn-up, then turn in the top edge by 1cm (⅜in) to neaten the raw edge. Insert Lonnie's legs into the jeans and then overstitch along the folded jeans edge just over the top of the leg to hold in place. This makes it neater and easier to attach the legs to the body.

01 Fold each jeans leg lengthwise and sew down the side seam. Turn under and sew the hem. If you want to be really fancy you could sew a machine stitch in yellow thread next to the pinking-sheared edge before you sew the seam, to give the impression of a selvedge edge when the jeans are turned up at the bottom. Drag your nail along the centre of the seam to press it open (it's a bit small and tricky to iron). Turn each leg to the right side.

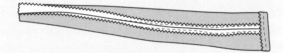

03. Using ladder stitch, attach the legs to the bottom of the body so they are close together in the centre. Denim is tricky to hand sew, so a nice sharp needle will help.

05. With right sides together, and using a small zigzag machine stitch, join the side seams of the front and back jumper pieces and the underarm seams on the sleeve pieces. Turn the sleeve pieces to the right side.

04. If you are using an existing jumper/T-shirt to make Lonnie's jumper, lay the front and back pattern pieces along its bottom edge – this will give you a finished edge so there is no need to hem. Do the same with the sleeves. If you are using a piece of knitted jersey fabric, add 3cm (1¼in) to the bottom of both patterns and then turn up and hem these edges by hand.

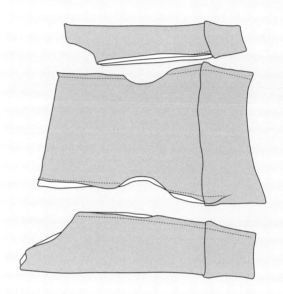

06 With right sides together and matching the underarm seams of the sleeves with the underarms of the body pieces, stitch the sleeves into the armholes using a small zigzag machine stitch. Turn to the right side.

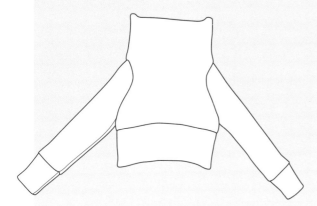

07 Fold down the neckline inside to where marked on the paper pattern, and then tack in position at the side seams. Dress Lonnie in his jumper – it's easier to put the jumper on from the legs up because his head is big.

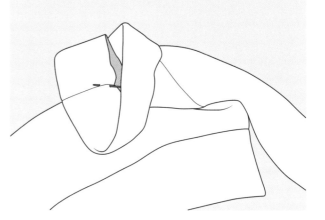

08

To make the scarf, on the woven fabric fray along two opposite edges by removing threads so the centre of the scarf measures 60 x 60cm (23⅝ x 23⅝in), not including the fringed edges. Divide the fringe into small sections and knot each section at the top. Double turn and machine stitch the other two edges. Fold the scarf into a triangle, then style around Lonnie's neck. You could buy a square scarf with frayed edges and cut it down to size – this way you will only have to fray and knot one of the edges.

SHAKKALOKKO

HEIGHT: 25CM (10IN)

Shakkalokko is a 1980s-based good-luck charm ideal for protecting your vinyl copy of *Now That's What I Call Music 3* or the stickers on your Rubik's Cube from scratches. Place him on your wall (ideally close to a copy of Cyndi Lauper's 1983 debut 'She's So Unusual') and bask in a comforting Magnum PI-style warmth.

YOU WILL NEED:

FELT
- Dark grey, 26 x 68cm (10¼ x 26¾in)
- Light grey, 15 x 8cm (6 x 3¼in)
- Pink, 15 x 12cm (6 x 4¾in)
- Aqua, 12 x 8cm (4¾ x 3¼in)
- Black, 3 x 5cm (1¼ x 2in)
- White, 2.5 x 4cm (1 x 1½in)

- 16mm (⅝in) black plastic safety eye
- 14mm (⁹⁄₁₆in) black plastic safety eye
- Small piece of cardboard (cereal box is perfect)
- 2oz wadding, 15 x 8cm (6 x 3¼in)
- Polyester fibre stuffing
- Small metal split ring approx 10mm (⅜in)

PATTERN PIECES:

- Head (cut 2 in dark grey felt)
- Gusset (cut 1 on fold on dark grey felt)
- Mouth (cut 1 in black felt)
- Upper teeth (cut 1 in white felt)
- Lower teeth (cut 1 in white felt)
- Face details 1, 4, 6, 8, 11, 13, 15, 16 (cut 1 in pink felt)
- Face details 2, 3, 5, 7, 9, 10, 12, 14 (cut 1 in aqua felt)
- Iris 1 (cut 1 in pink felt)
- Iris 2 (cut 1 in aqua felt)
- Eye 1 (cut 1 in card and 1 slightly bigger in both wadding and light grey felt)
- Eye 2 (cut 1 in card and 1 slightly bigger in both wadding and light grey felt)

01. Cut out all the pattern pieces in their corresponding fabrics.

02. Make up the eyes (see page 15) but don't attach them to the head yet.

03. Pin all the face details (except for the mouth and teeth) to one of the head pieces and slip stitch in place. Make sure the larger pieces overlap the ends of the small thin strips so they look neat. This is a bit of a puzzle, but use the paper patterns to see all placements.

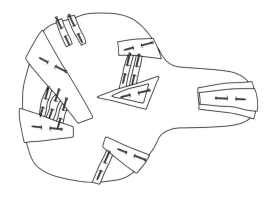

04. Attach the eyes to the face.

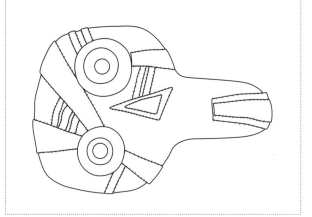

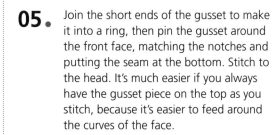

05. Join the short ends of the gusset to make it into a ring, then pin the gusset around the front face, matching the notches and putting the seam at the bottom. Stitch to the head. It's much easier if you always have the gusset piece on the top as you stitch, because it's easier to feed around the curves of the face.

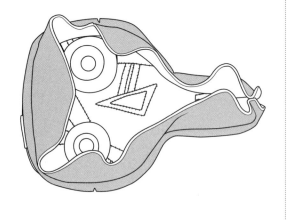

06.

Stitch the back of the head to the other edge of the gusset in the same way, but make sure you leave a gap for stuffing at the top. Turn to the right side and stuff, then use ladder stitch to close the gap left for stuffing.

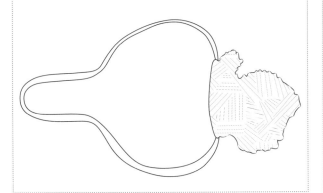

09.

Attach a metal ring to the back of the head so you can hang Shakkalokko up.

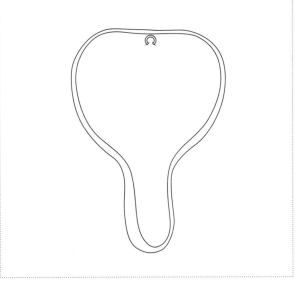

07.

Make up the mouth and then slip stitch to the head.

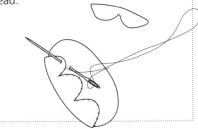

08.

Position the eyes and stitch around them with a slip stitch.

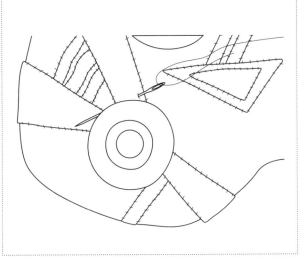

BERWYN & SCARP

HEIGHT: BERWYN 70CM (27½IN), SCARP 24CM (9½IN)

Berwyn is only happy when roaming the hills with his pet, Scarp. He can be spotted most days strolling over a drumlin, following an esker or clambering over moraine. Sometimes Berwyn lets Scarp off the lead while he sits on an erratic and writes one of his poems.

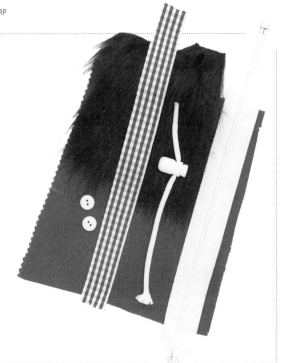

YOU WILL NEED:

For Berwyn
FELT
• Black, 35 x 45cm (14 x 18in)
• White, 12 x 6cm (4¾ x 2⅜in)

• Long-pile black fake fur, 60 x 60cm (23⅝ x 23⅝in)
• Pair of 16mm (⅝in) black plastic safety eyes
• 2 x 30mm (1¼in) plastic toy joints
• Small piece of cardboard (cereal box is perfect)
• 2oz wadding, 12 x 6cm (4¾ x 2⅜in)
• Polyester fibre stuffing
• Medium-weight cotton anorak fabric, 120 x 110cm (48 x 44in)
• 25cm (10in) white open-ended zip
• 4 x 12mm (½in) white buttons
• 2 x 25mm (1in) white plastic cylinder spring toggles
• 1m (1 yard) white cord

For Scarp
FELT
• Black felt, 15 x 15cm (6 x 6in)

• Long-pile black fake fur, 40 x 40cm (16 x 16in)
• Small piece of cardboard (cereal box is perfect)
• Pair of 20mm (¾in) black plastic eyes
• Polyester fibre stuffing
• 1m (40in) of 15mm (⅝in) ribbon
• Press stud (snap fastener) (optional)
• 16mm (⅝in) trigger hook
• 20mm (¾in) split ring

PATTERN PIECES:

BERWYN
• Body (cut 2 in fake fur)
• Arm (cut 2 in black felt)
• Leg (cut 2 in black felt)
• Foot pad (cut 2 in black felt)
• Toes (cut 4 in black felt)
• Base (cut 1 in black felt)
• Eye (cut 2 in card and 2 slightly bigger in both white felt and wadding)

BERWYN'S ANORAK
• Front (cut 2 in medium-weight cotton)
• Back (cut 1 on fold in medium-weight cotton)
• Sleeve (cut 2 in medium-weight cotton)
• Pocket (cut 2 in medium-weight cotton)
• Pocket flap (cut 4 in medium-weight cotton)
• Hood (cut 4 in medium-weight cotton)
• Hood gusset (cut 2 in medium-weight cotton)
• Front facing (cut 2 in medium-weight cotton)

SCARP
• Body (cut 2 in fake fur)
• Ear (cut 2 in fake fur)
• Tail (cut 1 in fake fur)
• Card base (cut 1 in card)
• Felt base (cut 1 in black felt)

01. Cut out all the pattern pieces in their corresponding fabrics and make holes for arms and eyes with a bradawl.

02. Make up the eyes (see page 15) and attach to the body.

03. Stitch the darts on the body shapes, tucking in any stray fibres as you sew. With right sides together, sew the two body pieces together, leaving the bottom edge unstitched.

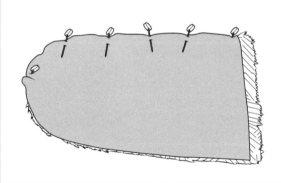

04. Pin the felt base into the bottom edge of the body, tucking stray fur fibres upwards out of the way, and stitch in place leaving a gap for stuffing as marked on the pattern.

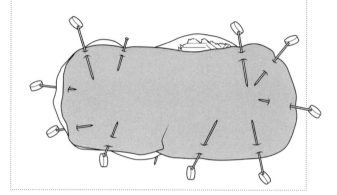

05. Fold each leg lengthwise and stitch down the longest edge. Pin the circular foot pad into the bottom of the leg, matching the quarters, and stitch in place. Turn to the right side and stuff.

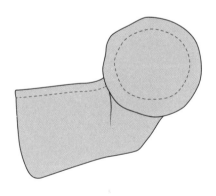

06. Sew around the sides and curved edge of the toes. Trim the excess fabric from around the stitching and nick in between the toes. Turn to the right side and stuff lightly.

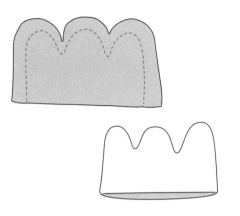

07. Tucking in the raw edge of each toe piece as you stitch, attach a set of toes to the bottom of each leg at the front, making sure the leg seam is at the back.

08. Fold each arm in half lengthwise and stitch down the longest edge and around the finger curves. Snip into the curves, then turn to the right side and stuff. Attach a joint to the top end of each arm and then attach to the body (see page 13).

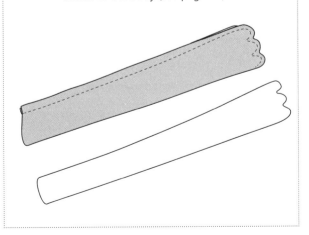

09. Stuff the body and then stitch up the gap using ladder stitch.

10. Ladder stitch the legs to the body base, making sure they are pointing forward.

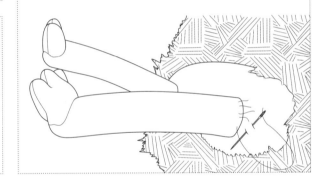

BERWYN'S ANORAK

01. Fold back and stitch the top of each pocket, then press the seam allowance inwards on the other three sides. Pin the pockets onto the anorak front where marked on the pattern and stitch in place.

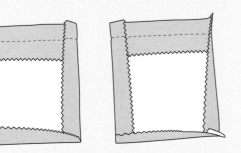

02. Place two pocket flap pieces right sides together and stitch around three edges. Cut across the corners and turn to the right side. Press flat and then topstitch around the finished edges, leaving the raw edge unstitched. Repeat for the other flap.

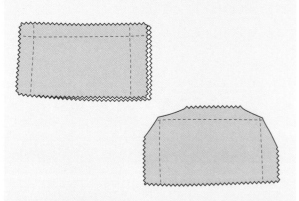

03. Pin a flap pointing upwards above each pocket on the anorak front and stitch into place. Press downwards.

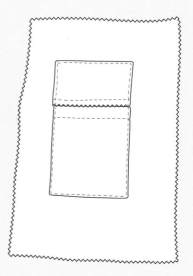

04. With right sides together and the gusset on the top as you sew, stitch a hood gusset between two hood pieces, matching the notches as you stitch. Repeat with the other gusset and two hood pieces to make the hood lining.

05. Pushing the seams inwards, topstitch along the hood gusset seam you have just stitched, so the topstitching sits on the gusset side of the seam.

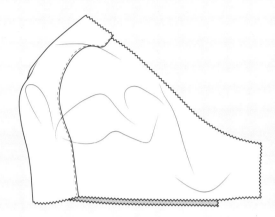

06. On the outer hood only, stitch the buttonholes where marked on the paper pattern.

07. With right sides together, stitch the front and back anorak pieces together, but just at the top of the side seams, above the upper notches, for approx 2cm (¾in).

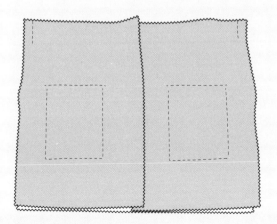

08. Open out the anorak pieces, folding the side seam you just stitched towards the back piece. With right sides together pin the top edge of one sleeve onto the anorak between the lower notches on the front and back pieces, matching the sleeve centre notch with the side seam position. Stitch from the sleeve centre notch to the lower notch on the front anorak piece only, stopping exactly at the lower notch. Then fold the side seam towards the front piece and stitch from the sleeve centre notch to the lower notch on the back anorak piece in the same way. Your stitching from the front and back lower notches should meet at the sleeve centre notch but not catch the side seam – this should remain free and unstitched underneath. Do the same with the other sleeve.

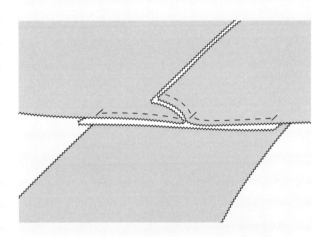

09. With right sides together fold the first sleeve in half, fold the front and back out of the way, and stitch the underarm seam from the wrist to the underarm. Again, be careful not to catch the anorak body front or back when stitching. At the underarm your stitching should exactly meet the end of the stitch line you made in step 08. Repeat on the other sleeve.

10. Stitch down the side seam from the underarm to the hemline on both sides, being careful not to catch the sleeve in the stitching. These last few stages require accuracy as all the stitched seams should meet up but not cross in any way. Turn the anorak and sleeves to the right side to check. The sleeve should be neatly attached with no pleats.

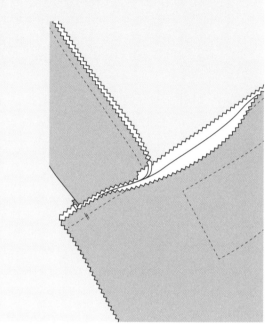

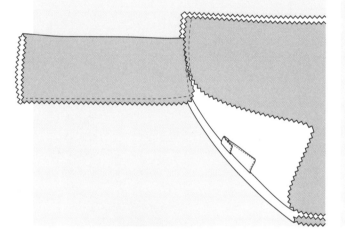

11. With right sides together stitch the hood piece with the buttonholes to the neckline of the anorak.

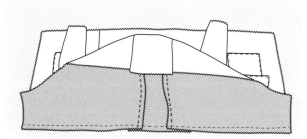

13. With right sides together, pin the zip to the front of the anorak on one side and stitch down using a zipper foot close to the teeth of the zip. The seam where the hood is attached should be pushed upwards out of the way.

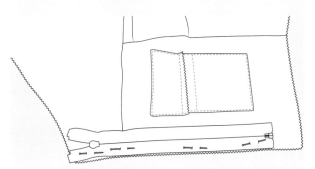

12. With right sides together stitch the front facings to the hood lining.

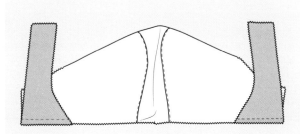

14. Before you stitch the other side of the zip into position mark it with a pin at the point where the hood seam lies. Unzip the other side of the zip and use the pin as a guide when pinning it to the other front piece so your seams will match up nicely when the zipper is fastened. Stitch in place.

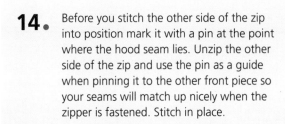

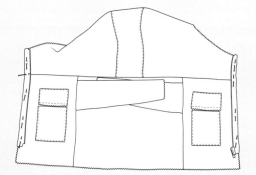

15. Pin the hood lining and front facing, with right sides together, to the anorak and stitch down the front and around the hood, still using your zipper foot.

17. Topstitch down the zip.

18. Topstitch from buttonhole to buttonhole, 1.5cm (⅝in) from the hood edge. This creates the channel for the hood cord.

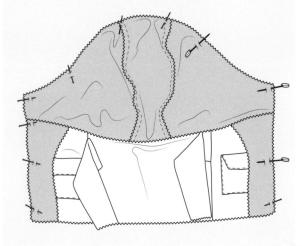

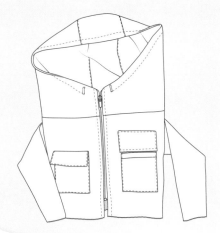

16. Topstitch/under stitch the seam on the hood lining and front facing. Press around the hood and front zip seam.

19. Double turn the hem as marked on the pattern, press and pin, then stitch.

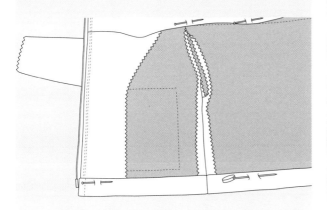

21. Wrap some sticky tape around each end of the cord to neaten it and prevent fraying, and attach one of the spring toggles. Attach a safety pin to the other end and use it to thread the cord through the buttonholes and around the hood channel. When it's through, remove the pin and attach the other spring toggle.

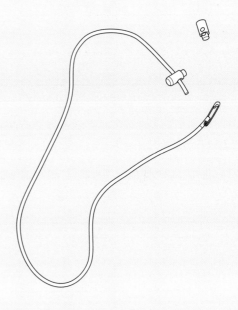

20. Turning the seam allowance under, slip stitch the hood lining to the anorak neckline.

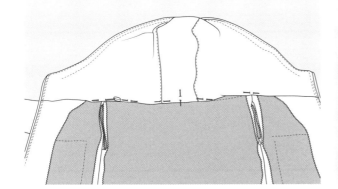

22. Sew buttons to the pocket flaps. If you want to secure these flaps, add a press stud to the centre.

23. Put the jacket onto Berwyn and then roll up his sleeves to the correct length.

SCARP

02. Turn to the right side and stuff the body.

01. Cut out all the pattern pieces in their corresponding fabrics and make holes for the eyes with a bradawl. Stitch the darts and side seams as you did for Berwyn. Attach the plastic safety eyes (see page 15).

03. Sew running stitch around the circumference of the felt base piece and gather the thread until the felt base fits neatly around the card case piece. Pin to the bottom of the body and ladder stitch in place.

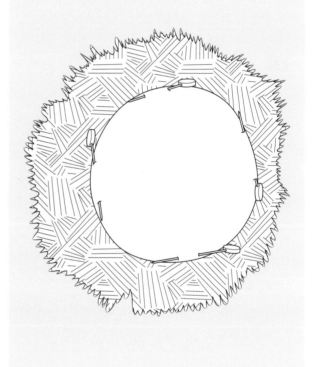

04. Fold the edges of the ears to the centre and overstitch along the top edge. Pin the ears to the top of the head and ladder stitch in place.

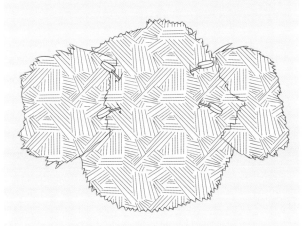

06. To make the collar, cut 48cm (18⅞in) of ribbon, fold over the ends twice to cover the raw edges and attach a press stud (follow the manufacturer's instructions as they can differ) over the ends. Thread on the split ring and then fit the collar to Scarp's neck.

05. With wrong sides together, fold the tail and overstitch the two raw edges together. Ladder stitch to the body at the centre back near the base.

07. Take the remaining 52cm of ribbon and fold the ends in by 1cm (⅜in). Thread on the spring hook at one end and secure with stitches, either by hand or machine. Fold the other end down by 5cm (2in) and stitch to make a loop.

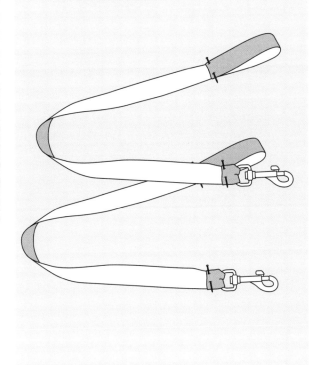

PIPPA TRIPP & POM

HEIGHT: PIPPA 105CM (42IN), POM 12CM (4¾IN)

Pippa's first novel, *The Gribbled Wig*, was an instant best-seller (later made into a film starring furry heartthrob, Gombo Wappling) and a hit with critics worldwide. Her following novels are all equally successful and tackled subjects as diverse as robotic whippets, limescale and paper cuts. She's never without her pet/muse, Pom.

YOU WILL NEED:

For Pippa Tripp
FELT
- Aqua, 50 x 75cm (20 x 30in)
- Dark blue, 45 x 40cm (18 x 16in)
- Black, 17 x 12cm (6¾ x 4¾in)
- White, 10 x 7.5cm (4 x 3in)
- Pink, 61 x 10cm (24½ x 4in)

- Long-pile blue fake fur, 61 x 50cm (24½ x 20in)
- Pair of 14mm (⁹⁄₁₆in) black safety eyes
- 2 x 30mm (1¼in) plastic toy joints
- Polyester fibre stuffing
- Dress fabric (rayon, lightweight cotton or viscose), 80 x 110cm (32 x 44in)
- 4 x 6mm (¼in) press studs (snaps)
- 30mm (1¼in) belt buckle
- Ric-rac braid, 2m (2 yards)
- Small pieces of cardboard, slightly stiffer than a cereal box
- Small pieces of corrugated cardboard
- Stretch fabric (I used part of a coloured sock), 21 x 6cm (8⅜ x 2⅜in)

For Pom
FELT
- White, 5 x 7cm (2 x 2¾in)
- Black, 2.5 x 2.5cm (1 x 1in)
- Dark blue, 15 x 3.5cm (6 x 1½in)

- Long-pile blue fake fur, 30 x 32cm (12 x 12⅝in)
- Pair of 12mm (½in) black plastic eyes
- Small piece of cardboard (cereal box is perfect)
- Polyester fibre stuffing
- 50cm (20in) of chain for the lead

PATTERN PIECES:

PIPPA TRIPP
- Head (cut 2 in fake fur)
- Upper body (cut 2 in aqua felt)
- Lower body (cut 2 in dark blue felt)
- Base (cut 1 in dark blue felt)
- Leg (cut 2 in aqua felt)
- Foot (cut 4 in aqua felt)
- Arm (cut 2 in aqua felt)
- Fingers (cut 2 in pink felt)
- Toenails (cut 2 of each of the three sizes marked on pattern in pink felt)
- Eye (cut 2 in black felt)
- Eye white (cut 2 in white felt)
- Eyeliner (cut 2 in pink felt)
- Teeth (cut 1 in white felt)
- Mouth (cut 1 in black felt)

PIPPA'S DRESS AND SHOES
- Bodice front (cut 1 in dress fabric)
- Bodice back (cut 2 in dress fabric)
- Sleeve (cut 2 in dress fabric)
- Sleeve lining (cut 2 in dress fabric)
- Skirt: no pattern, cut a rectangle 25 x 110cm (10 x 44in)
- Collar (cut 1 on fold in dress fabric)
- Bow (cut 1 on fold in dress fabric)
- Bow knot (cut 1 in dress fabric)
- Belt (cut 1 on fold in pink felt)
- Shoe card (cut 4 in stiff card and 8 in corrugated card)
- Shoe sole (cut 4 in dark blue felt)
- Shoe strap (cut 2 in stretch fabric)

POM
- Body (cut 4 in fake fur)
- Eye (cut 2 in card and 2 slightly bigger in white felt)
- Mouth (cut 1 in black felt)
- Teeth (cut 1 in white felt)
- Lead handle (cut 1 in dark blue felt)
- Strip to join chain to handle (cut 1 in dark blue felt)

01. Cut out all the pattern pieces in their corresponding fabrics and make holes for the arms and eyes with a bradawl. Use a craft knife to cut the slit in the eye pieces.

02. With right sides together join the head, upper body and lower body on both sets of pieces, making sure on one set you leave the gap for stuffing on the head/upper body seam as marked on the pattern.

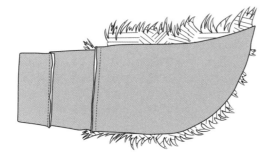

03. Pin both sets with right sides together, pushing in any stray fur fibres as you pin. Starting at the point on the head (so you are always stitching down the fur pile), stitch down both sides.

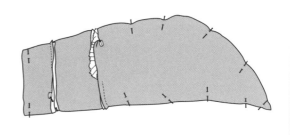

04. Pin the felt base piece to the bottom of the body, matching notches, and stitch in place. Turn to the right side.

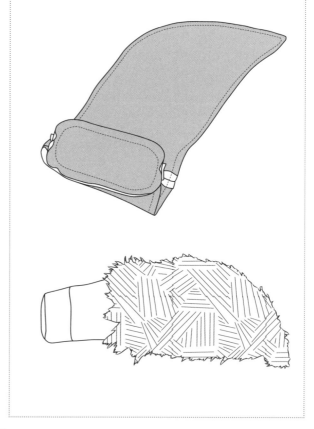

05. Insert the top of the eye white into the slit made in the eye piece, then push a plastic eye through the hole in the eye white and eye and then into the body, securing with the washer on the inside. Slip stitch the eyeliner onto the eye along the top edge of the slit. Then slip stitch around the eye onto the body, leaving the eyelashes unstitched. (These are done in a similar way to Lottie's eyes, so check her instructions if you need more help.) Repeat for the other eye.

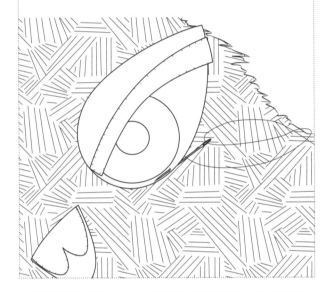

06. Slip stitch the teeth to the mouth, then slip stitch the mouth onto the head.

07. Fold each arm lengthwise and insert the finger pieces into the bottom straight edge pointing inwards. Stitch across to secure and then stitch down and around the end, leaving a gap for stuffing. Turn to the right side, insert the plastic joints (see page 13) and stuff. Stitch the gap closed and then attach the arms to the body with the joints.

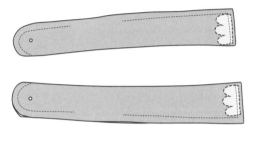

08. Stuff the body/head and ladder stitch the gap closed.

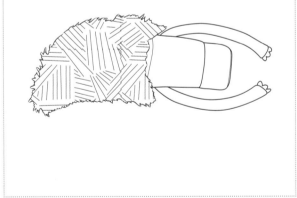

09. Fold the legs in half lengthwise and stitch down the longest edge. Turn to the right side and stuff. Sew running stitch around the top edge of each leg and pull tight to close, securing the thread with a few stitches. Repeat on the bottom edge of each leg.

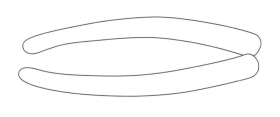

11. Using ladder stitch, attach a foot to the end of each leg, making sure the leg seams are at the back. The legs should neatly cover the cut cross used to turn the feet through.

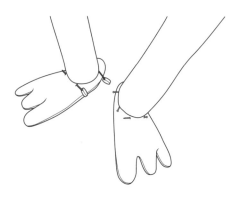

10. Sew the feet pieces together to make a pair of feet. Trim around close to the stitching and nick in between the toes. Turn to the right side through the cut cross (as marked on pattern). Stuff lightly. On the other side of the feet, slip stitch on the toenails.

12. Ladder stitch the legs to the body base where marked on the pattern.

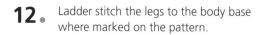

PIPPA'S DRESS

03. On the sleeve, gather the bottom edge between the notches, either by stitching two rows of running stitch and pulling the threads or by using a gathering foot on your machine. It should be gathered to the same width as the bottom edge of the sleeve lining piece.

01. Sew a small bow onto the upper and lower body seam at the centre front to give the impression of underwear.

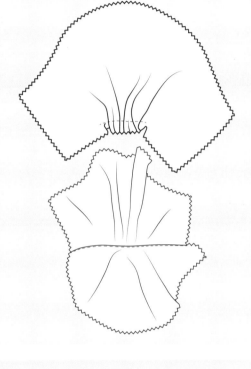

02. Join the side seams on the bodice, on either side of the armholes, and press the seams open.

04. Join the underarm seam of the sleeve and, matching the seams, continue down the sleeve lining. Drag your nail along the centre of this seam to keep it open, as it's too tricky to press open with the iron.

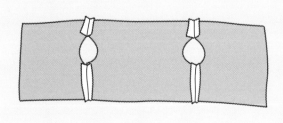

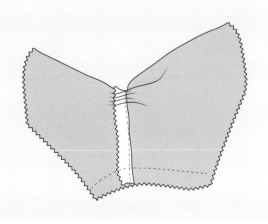

05. Pin the sleeve lining head to the sleeve head and tack in place. Gather the sleeve head between the notches – about 2.5cm (1in). The lining is shorter than the outer sleeve, so when tacked together and gathered they make the sleeve 'puff'.

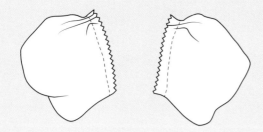

07. Fold the collar strip lengthwise, right sides together, and sew down the two short ends. Cut across the corners and turn to the right side. Press along the folded edge and pin the two raw edges together. Pin this strip, right sides together, so it's centred on the bodice at the neck edge. Wrap the ends of the bodice over as marked on the pattern to form front facings, and stitch in place all along the neck edge.

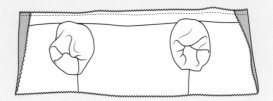

06. With right sides together and matching the underarm seams, insert and stitch the sleeves into the armholes. This is quite fiddly so if you find it tricky to sew on the machine, hand sew using a small back stitch.

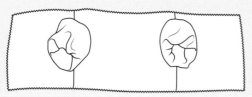

08. Make the skirt. With right sides together, join the short edges leaving 6cm (2⅜in) from the top unstitched – this will be the centre back. With a pin or notch, mark the point opposite the seam at the top of the skirt – this will be the centre front, which will help you get the gathers even when attaching to the bodice. Sew two rows of running stitch along the top edge, pulling the threads to gather so the skirt fits the bottom edge of the bodice.

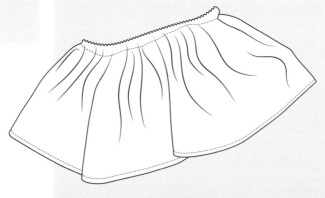

09. Attach the skirt to the bodice, matching the pin to the centre front notch on the bodice, and folding the back bodice facings back over the skirt as you stitch. Hem the skirt.

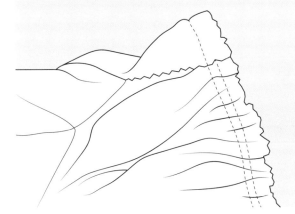

10. Fold the bow in half lengthwise with right sides together and stitch all around the raw edges, leaving a gap of 4cm (1½in). Turn to the right side and press.

11. Fold the bow in half, pin a line across the centre, and then stitch along this pinned line. Open out the ends and flatten the centre loop evenly over the stitched seam.

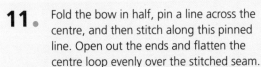

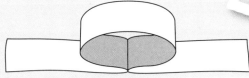

12. Make a second line of stitching to gather up the bow across the centre.

13. Fold the bow knot in half lengthwise, right sides together, and stitch the long edge. Turn to the right side and press flat with the seam in the centre.

15. Using a few small stitches, attach the bow to the left side of the dress near the shoulder.

16. Fold one end of the felt belt piece over the belt buckle bar and secure with a few small stitches.

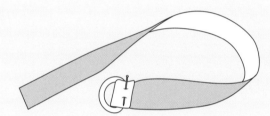

14. Fold right sides together again and stitch across the raw ends. Turn to the right side and thread the bow through the bow knot.

17. Stitch the press studs onto the back bodice. Check the fit of the dress on Pippa before you do this, because the press studs can easily be positioned to make the dress a little tighter or looser if needed.

PIPPA'S SHOES

01. Put a stiff shoe card and a corrugated shoe card together with the holes aligned. Sew a row of running stitches around the edge of the felt shoe sole and pull tightly to fit neatly around them, with the stiff card next to the felt. Repeat, making sure you have a left and a right shoe. With a bradawl, make a hole in each felt piece to match the hole in the card. These are the shoe upper soles.

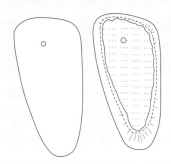

02. Place three of the remaining corrugated shoe cards and one stiff shoe card together, and cover these with a felt shoe sole in the same way, again with the stiff card nearest the felt. Make sure you are using strong thread because there are multiple layers of card and you need to pull the gathers in tight. Repeat, making sure you have a left and a right shoe. If you are worried about the card pieces slipping while you sew, stick them together first with double-sided tape. These are the shoe bottom soles.

03. Push the centre of a shoe strap fabric piece through the hole in the felt side of a shoe upper sole, using a chopstick or knitting needle. On the underside, secure the centre of the strap to the felt on either side with some large stitches. Pin the ends of the straps to the felt on the underside of the sole (see markings on paper pattern). How tight you attach them depends on the size of your character's feet so try them on Pippa for size before stitching. They should be quite tight as they are cut from stretch fabric. When you are happy with the fit, secure with a few small stitches underneath. Repeat for the second shoe.

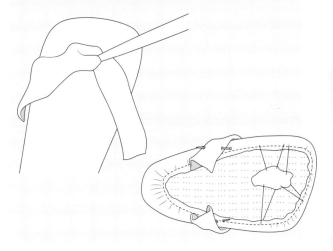

04. Place the upper sole on the bottom sole, with wrong sides together, and sew together with ladder stitch. Slip stitch ric-rac braid over the join to hide the ladder stitching.

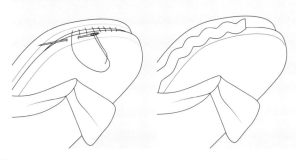

POM

01. Cut out all the pattern pieces in their corresponding fabrics. Stitch the darts in all four body pieces, then snip open along the fold and press each dart out flat. Stitch each pair of pieces right sides together along the edges without darts, leaving a gap for stuffing in one seam.

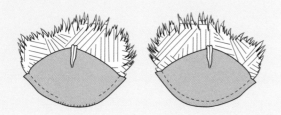

02. Matching up darts and seams and tucking in any stray fur fibres as you stitch, join the two halves all around the edge. Turn to the right side.

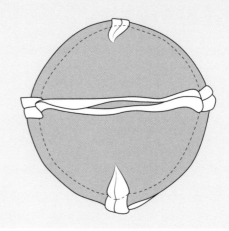

03. Make up and attach the eyes (see page 15). Pom's eyes have no wadding, just felt-covered card. Stuff the body, and then ladder stitch the gap closed.

04. Thread the small strip of felt through the end of the chain, and then fold the felt lead handle piece over the ends of this felt strip and stitch across to secure.

05. Stitch the other end of the chain to Pom at the side seam and in line with the eyes.

ABOUT THE AUTHOR

From her studio in North Wales, Felt Mistress has created a legion of felt characters for the best part of a decade. Felt Mistress, aka Louise Evans, is a UK-based stitcher and prolific tea drinker who creates a range of one-off bespoke creatures with her partner, illustrator Jonathan Edwards. In 2010 they were given their own window in Selfridges' iconic Oxford Street store as part of the Christmas display and were the focal point of the store's world-famous Wonder Room. In 2011 they spent six weeks in Japan creating work for a gallery residency in Nara, which culminated in headlining the Headspace arts festival in Osaka. *Felt Mistress: Creature Couture*, containing all their work to date, was published in 2012. Their work has been exhibited all over the world, including shows in Osaka, Los Angeles, Berlin and London, and used in ad campaigns, fashion shoots, music videos and films.

Louise trained in fashion design and millinery and brings many of the skills learned through years of work as a couture dressmaker to the world of character design. As well as original Felt Mistress characters, Louise has also collaborated with a variety of other artists including Jon Burgerman, Ben Newman, Pete Fowler and Gruff Rhys.

THANK YOU

To my friends and family,
and especially
Jonathan Edwards,
Jon Burgerman
and Pete Fowler.